LITERACY SK...

Grammar ...nd punctuation

Year 3

TERMS AND CONDITIONS

IMPORTANT – PERMITTED USE AND WARNINGS – READ CAREFULLY BEFORE USING

Minimum system requirements:

- PC or Mac with CD-ROM drive (16x speed recommended) and 512MB RAM
- P4 or G4 processor
- Windows 2000/XP/Vista or Mac OSX 10.3 or later

For all technical support queries, please phone Scholastic Customer Services on 0845 6039091.

Author

Huw Thomas

Editor

Rachel Mackinnon

Assistant editors

Vicky Butt and Louise Titley

CD-ROM design and development team

Joy Monkhouse, Anna Oliwa,
Micky Pledge, Rebecca Male, Allison Parry,
Sean Parkes /Beehive Illustration and Haremi

Series designers

Shelley Best and Anna Oliwa

Book design team

Shelley Best and Sonja Bagley

Illustrations

Jane Cope

Designed using Adobe Indesign
Published by Scholastic Ltd, Villiers House,
Clarendon Avenue, Leamington Spa,
Warwickshire CV32 5PR
www.scholastic.co.uk

Printed by Bell & Bain Ltd, Glasgow
Text © 1999, 2008 Huw Thomas
© 2008 Scholastic Ltd
1 2 3 4 5 6 7 8 9 0 8 9 0 1 2 3 4 5 6 7

British Library Cataloguing-in-Publication Data
A catalogue record for this book is available from
the British Library.
ISBN 978-1407-10046-3

Acknowledgements

The publishers gratefully acknowledge permission to reproduce
the following copyright material:

The Agency (London) Ltd for the use of a poem 'Our Car' by
Tony Bradman from *Things that go* by Tony Bradman © 1989,
Tony Bradman (1989, Blackie). **Andersen Press** for the use of an
extract from *Way Home* by Libby Hathorn © 1994, Libby Hathorn
(1994, Random House Australia). **Gerald Duckworth & Co Ltd**
for the use of 'Overheard on the saltmarsh' by Harold Munro from
Collected Poems by Harold Munro © 1970, Harold Munro (1970,
Gerald Duckworth). **The Literary Trustees of Walter de la Mare
and the Society of Authors** as their representatives for use of
'The Listeners' by Walter de la Mare from *The Complete Poems of
Walter de la Mare* © 1912, Walter de la Mare (reprinted 1975, Faber
and Faber). **Peters Fraser and Dunlop Group Ltd** for the use of
an extract from *Granny* by Anthony Horowitz © 1994, Anthony
Horowitz (1994, Walker Books). **Walker Books** for an extract
from *Farmer Duck* by Martin Waddell © 1991, Martin Waddell
(1991, Walker Books); for an extract from *Where's my teddy?* by
Jez Alborough © 1992, Jez Alborough (1992, Walker Books) and
an extract from *Owl Babies* by Martin Waddell © 1992, Martin
Waddell (1992, Walker Books).

Every effort has been made to trace copyright holders for the
works reproduced in this book, and the publishers apologise for
any inadvertent omissions.

Extracts from Primary National Strategy's Primary Framework for
Literacy (2006) www.standards.dfes.gov.uk/primaryframework ©
Crown copyright. Reproduced under the terms of the Click Use
Licence.

Contents

Chapter 1
Nouns and pronouns

Chapter 2
Pronouns

Chapter 3
Adjectives

Chapter 4
Verbs

Chapter 5
Making sentences

Chapter 6
Sentence writing and conjunctions

Introduction

The Scholastic Literacy Skills: Grammar and punctuation series

This series works from the premise that grammar and punctuation can be interesting and dynamic – but on one condition. The condition is that the teaching of these aspects of grammar must be related to real texts and practical activities that experiment with language, investigate the use of language in real contexts and find the ways in which grammar and punctuation are used in our day-to-day talk, writing and reading. This book encourages children to look back at their written work and find ways to revise and improve it.

Teaching grammar and punctuation

'As a writer I know that I must select studiously the nouns, pronouns, verbs, adverbs, etcetera, and by a careful syntactical arrangement make readers laugh, reflect or riot.'
Maya Angelou

The *Scholastic Literacy Skills: Grammar and punctuation* series equips teachers with resources and subject training enabling them to teach grammar and punctuation. The focus of the resource is on what is sometimes called sentence-level work, so called because grammar and punctuation primarily involve the construction and understanding of sentences.

Many teachers bring with them a lot of past memories when they approach the teaching of grammar. Some will remember school grammar lessons as the driest of subjects, involving drills and parsing, and will wonder how they can make it exciting for their own class. At the other end of the spectrum, some will have received relatively little formal teaching of grammar at school. In other words, there are teachers who, when asked to teach clause structure or prepositions, feel at a bit of a loss. They are being asked to teach things they are not confident with themselves. Even worse, they think they should be confident in these things.

Grammar can evoke lethargy, fear, irritation, pedantry and despondency. Yet as can be seen from the above comment by Maya Angelou, we have one of the greatest modern writers presenting her crafting of sentences as an exciting and tactical process that has a powerful effect on her readers. Can this be the grammar that makes teachers squirm or run?

About the product

The book is divided into six chapters. Each chapter looks at a different aspect of grammar and punctuation and is divided into five sections. Each section includes teachers' notes – objective, background knowledge, notes on how to use the photocopiable pages, further ideas and what's on the CD-ROM – and two to three photocopiable pages.

Posters

Each chapter has two posters. These posters are related to the contents of the chapter and should be displayed and used for reference throughout the work on the chapter. The poster notes (on the chapter opening page) offer suggestions for how they could be used. There are black and white versions in the book and full-colour versions on the CD-ROM for you to print out or display on your whiteboard.

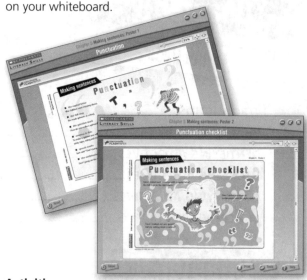

Activities

Each section contains two to three activities. These activities all take the form of a photocopiable page which is in the book. Each photocopiable page is also included on the CD-ROM for you to display or print out (these pages also provide answers where appropriate). Over thirty of the photocopiable pages have linked interactive activities on the CD-ROM. These interactive activities are designed to act as starter activities to the lesson, giving whole-class support on the information being taught. However, they can also work equally well as plenary activities, reviewing the work the children have just completed.

Getting started

To begin using the CD-ROM, simply place it in your CD- or DVD-ROM drive. Although the CD-ROM should auto-run, if it fails to do so, navigate to the drive and double-click on the red **Start** icon.

Start-up screen

The start-up screen is the first screen that appears. Here you can access: terms and conditions, registration links, how to use the CD-ROM and credits. If you agree to the terms and conditions, click **Start** to continue.

Main menu

The main menu provides links to all of the chapters or all of the resources. Clicking on the relevant **Chapter** icon will take you to the chapter screen where you can access the posters and the chapter's sections. Clicking on **All resources** will take you to a list of all the resources, where you can search by key word or chapter for a specific resource.

Writing sections

The final section in each chapter focuses on writing. It differs slightly in layout to the other sections – rather than teaching children new skills, you are encouraging them to practise the ones they have already learned throughout the chapter and to use them in writing. There are two photocopiable pages in each of these sections; many of them are writing frames or provide prompts to encourage the children to write. As with the other sections, a number of further ideas are also included, which provide imaginative and interesting starting points for writing.

Using the CD-ROM

Below are brief guidance notes for using the CD-ROM. For more detailed information, see **How to use** on the start-up screen, or **Help** on the relevant screen for information about that page.

The CD-ROM follows the structure of the book and contains:

- All of the photocopiable pages.
- All of the poster pages in full colour.
- Photocopiable pages (with answers where appropriate).
- Over thirty interactive on-screen activities linked to the photocopiable pages.

Section screen

Upon choosing a section from the chapter screen, you are taken to a list of resources for that section. Here you can access all of the photocopiable pages related to that section as well as the linked interactive activities.

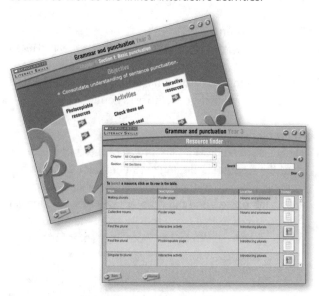

Resource finder

The **Resource finder** lists all of the resources on the CD-ROM. You can:

- Select a chapter and/or section by selecting the appropriate title from the drop-down menus.
- Search for key words by typing them into the search box.
- Scroll up or down the list of resources to locate the required resource.
- To launch a resource, simply click on its row on the screen.

Navigation

The resources (poster pages, photocopiable pages and interactive activities) all open in separate windows on top of the menu screen. This means that you can have more than one resource open at the same time. To close a resource, click on the **x** in the top right-hand corner of the screen. To return to the menu screen you can either close or minimise a resource.

Closing a resource will not close the program. However, if you are in a menu screen, then clicking on the **x** will close the program. To return to a previous menu screen, you need to click on the **Back** button.

Glossary

Most of the interactive activities link to a glossary. The glossary will open in a separate window. Simply click first on the desired headletter and then on the word to reveal its definition.

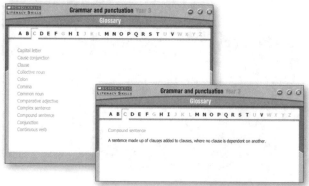

Whiteboard tools

The CD-ROM comes with its own set of whiteboard tools for use on any whiteboard. These include:

- Pen tool
- Highlighter tool
- Eraser
- Sticky note

Click on the **Tools** button at the foot of the screen to access these tools.

Printing

Print the resources by clicking on the **Print** button. The photocopiable pages print as full A4 portrait pages, but please note if you have a landscape photocopiable page or poster you need to set the orientation to landscape in your print preferences. The interactive activities will print what is on the screen. For a full A4 printout you need to set the orientation to landscape in your print preferences.

Framework objectives

Chapter	Page	Section	Literacy skills objective	Strand 6: Recognise a range of prefixes and suffixes, understanding how they modify meaning and spelling, and how they assist in decoding long complex words.	Strand 11: Show relationships of time, reason and cause through subordination and connectives.	Strand 11: Compose sentences using adjectives, verbs and nouns for precision, clarity and impact.	Strand 11: Clarify meaning through the use of exclamation marks and speech marks.
Chapter 1	12	Introducing plurals	Recognise the use of singular and plural nouns.	✓		✓	
	16	Collective nouns	Understand and recognise the use of collective nouns.			✓	
	20	Person	Understand the need for grammatical agreement.	✓		✓	
	24	Pronouns take their place	Substitute pronouns for nouns.			✓	
	28	Writing with nouns and pronouns	Understand and apply the concept of person in relation to nouns.	✓		✓	
Chapter 2	35	Pronouns	Identify pronouns.			✓	
	39	Two types of pronouns	Distinguish personal and possessive pronouns.			✓	
	43	Different types of pronouns	Distinguish first-, second- and third-person pronouns.			✓	
	47	Pronouns in text	Investigate the use of pronouns.			✓	
	51	Pronouns in writing	To extend the use of pronouns in writing.			✓	
Chapter 3	58	What is an adjective?	Define the function of adjectives.			✓	
	62	Identify adjectives	Identify adjectives.			✓	
	66	Changing adjectives	Experimenting with substituting adjectives in sentences.			✓	
	70	Classifying adjectives	Collect and classify adjectives.			✓	
	74	Adjectives in writing	To refine the use of adjectives in writing			✓	

Framework objectives

			Strand 6: Recognise a range of prefixes and suffixes, understanding how they modify meaning and spelling, and how they assist in decoding long complex words.	Strand 11: Show relationships of time, reason and cause through subordination and connectives.	Strand 11: Compose sentences using adjectives, verbs and nouns for precision, clarity and impact.	Strand 11: Clarify meaning through the use of exclamation marks and speech marks.
Page	**Section**	**Literacy skills objective**				
Chapter 4						
81	Collecting verbs	Learn the function of verbs in sentences, observing their key role in sentences.				
85	Changing verbs	Understand and recognise the use of collective nouns.			✓	
89	Tenses	Understand the need for grammatical agreement.	✓		✓	
93	Investigating verbs	Learn to consider the function of verbs in sentences.				
97	Verbs in writing	To expand children's use of verbs in writing.			✓	
Chapter 5						
104	Basic punctuation	Consolidate understanding of sentence punctuation.				✓
108	Commas and inverted commas	Apply punctuation in writing. Learn to use commas in lists and inverted commas.				✓
112	Speech marks	Use speech marks and other dialogue punctuation.			✓	✓
116	Sentences working together	Use commas to mark grammatical boundaries in sentences.			✓	✓
120	Punctuation in writing	Apply punctuation in writing.				✓
Chapter 6						
127	Time words	Investigate how words and phrases signal time.		✓		
131	Conjunctions	Use a wider range of conjunctions in extending sentences.		✓		
135	Sentences making sense	Develop awareness of longer sentences through experimenting with the deletion of words. Understand the use of commas in longer sentences.			✓	✓
139	Working with sentences	Consolidate an understanding of sentences.		✓	✓	
143	Improving sentence writing	Write more extended sentences.		✓	✓	

Chapter 1

Nouns and pronouns

Introduction

This chapter focuses on nouns and pronouns, considering the formation of plurals, the nature of collective nouns and the way in which pronouns substitute for nouns. Throughout there is an emphasis on the concept of 'person' and nature of grammatical agreement. The chapter ends with an application of these grammatical features to writing, including looking at the place of nouns in report texts.

In this chapter

Introducing plurals page 12	Recognise the use of singular and plural nouns.
Collective nouns page 16	Understand and recognise the use of collective nouns.
Person page 20	Understand the need for grammatical agreement.
Pronouns take their place page 24	Substitute pronouns for nouns.
Writing with nouns and pronouns page 28	Understand and apply the concept of person in relation to nouns.

Poster notes

Making plurals (page 10)

This poster provides a reference point throughout the chapter, but particularly in 'Introducing plurals'. The table is used to show the ways in which plurals are made. The point to stress is that the usual rule is to add 's' to a noun to make a plural but that there are exceptions to this rule. The poster should be kept on display for children to refer to as they form plurals in their independent work.

Collective nouns (page 11)

The poster provides a list of collective nouns and will support work in 'Collective nouns'. Some are better known than others. Children can draw on examples on the poster while adding to their repertoire of collective nouns.

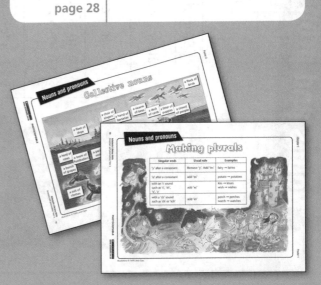

Nouns and pronouns

Making plurals

Singular ends	Usual rule	Examples
'y' after a consonant	Remove 'y'. Add 'ies'	fairy → fairies
'o' after a consonant	add 'es'	potato → potatoes
with an 's' sound such as 's', 'sh', 'x', 'z'	add 'es'	kiss → kisses wish → wishes
with a 'ch' sound such as 'ch' or 'tch'	add 'es'	perch → perches watch → watches

Illustrations © 2008, Jane Cope.

PHOTOCOPIABLE

SCHOLASTIC
www.scholastic.co.uk

Nouns and pronouns

Collective nouns

a flock of birds

a crowd of people

a litter of puppies

a deck of cards

a swarm of bees

a hand of bananas

a choir of singers

a fleet of ships

a herd of cows

a team of footballers

a bunch of grapes

a pack of wolves

a crew of sailors

a school of whales

a stack of hay

a forest of trees

a staff of teachers

a suit of clothes

Illustrations © 2008, Jane Cope.

Introducing plurals

Objective

Recognise the use of singular and plural nouns.

Background knowledge

A plural denotes more than one of a noun, whether it be a single item or a single collection of lots of items (a collective noun). The usual rule for turning a singular noun into a plural is to add an 's' (as in cows, videos and pieces) but there are some exceptions to this rule. The way in which a singular noun is adapted to make a plural depends on the ending of the singular. The exceptions are shown below.

Singular ends	Usual rule	Example
'y' after a consonant	Remove 'y'. Add 'ies'	fairy → fairies
'o' after a consonant	add 'es'	potato → potatoes
with an 's' sound such as 's', 'sh', x', 'z'	add 'es'	kiss → kisses wish → wishes
with a 'ch' sound such as 'ch', 'tch'	add 'es'	perch → perches watch → watches

Activities

The rule of adding 's' except when faced with an exception to the rule is a key element of children learning to form plural nouns correctly. Children need to practise noticing nouns that result in exceptions.

● **Photocopiable page 13 'Find the plural'**
As children match singular and plural nouns, this activity can result in them looking for the general rule of adding an 's' and noticing some of the exceptions. The activity can be adapted by writing the singular and plural nouns on cards and asking the children to match them (see 'Cards' in Further ideas).

● **Photocopiable page 14 'Singular to plural'**
As they change these sentences, children will notice that there are certain words they need to change and certain words that stay the same.

● **Photocopiable page 15 'Hints about plurals'**
This activity provides a straightforward introduction to the effect that pluralisation has on the spelling of certain words. It introduces children to the chart of exceptions to the general rule of adding an 's'.

Further ideas

● **Cards:** Using the nouns from photocopiable page 13 'Find the plural' and other singular/plural nouns, a set of cards can be made showing the singular and plural of a set of nouns. Children can try to match these up. As new nouns are introduced to the class they can be added to the card pack.
● **Shared text:** As the class shares a text they can look out for singular and plural nouns they encounter along the way.
● **Unusual plurals:** Children can keep a collection of plurals that are exceptions to the general rule of adding an 's'.

What's on the CD-ROM

On the CD-ROM you will find:
● Printable versions of all three photocopiable pages.
● Answers to all three photocopiable pages.
● Interactive versions of all three photocopiable pages.

Introducing plurals

Find the plural

■ Look at these words. Find their plurals. Write them in the plural space.

Singular	Plural
child	children
fish	
woman	
mouse	
school	
house	
friend	
foot	
fox	
leaf	
potato	
class	
dress	
box	
branch	
dog	
girl	
teacher	
switch	

houses

dresses   branches

dogs
                            potatoes
leaves

          teachers
                        classes

children
                            feet
          boxes

schools   fish

          friends
                    girls

foxes
          switches

women   mice

■ Use **two** of the singular nouns in sentences.

_____

_____

■ Use **two** of the plural nouns in sentences.

_____

_____

Name:

Introducing plurals

Singular to plural

■ Look at these sentences. The nouns are singular. Can you rewrite the sentences with plurals? You may need to change other words to suit the plurals.

The pirate talked to the parrot.		
The girl played with her football.		
The clown fell off the bike.		
My friend ate the potato.		
You use the switch to turn on the light.		
Don't lose the key for the cupboard.		
I can make a cake with a cherry on top.		
The dog chased the teacher up the tree.		
The princess found her dress in the box.		
The leaf fell from a branch of the tree.		
The girl had a sweet.		

Illustrations © 1999, Jane Cope.

PHOTOCOPIABLE

Name:

Introducing plurals

Hints about plurals

We make plurals by adding 's' to a noun except when:

Singular ends	Usual rule	Examples
'y' after a consonant	Remove 'y'. Add 'ies'	fairy → fairies
'o' after a consonant	add 'es'	potato → potatoes
with an 's' sound such as 's', 'sh', 'x', 'z'	add 'es'	kiss → kisses wish → wishes
with a 'ch' sound such as 'ch', 'tch'	add 'es'	perch → perches watch → watches

■ Try making the plurals for these words.

Singular	Plural
diary	
nappy	
tomato	
rodeo	
cross	
crutch	
church	
splash	
tray	
watch	
hutch	
porch	
hiss	
mess	
puppy	
ranch	
crash	

Illustrations © 1999, Jane Cope.

Collective nouns

Objective

Understand and recognise the use of collective nouns.

Background knowledge

Collective nouns are used to denote a group of items, such as a bunch of bananas or a flock of sheep. Collections are single items, but they can also be pluralised (meaning more than one collection of items), as in *flocks of sheep*.

There is a small number of commonly-used collective nouns that children will encounter.

Activities

Once children have grasped the idea of a collective noun, share as many examples as possible.

● **Photocopiable page 17 'A pile of guesses'**
Some of these collective nouns will be known to the children. Some will require an element of guesswork. The correct pairings are in the table on the right.

● **Photocopiable page 18 'Make up collective nouns'**
As children create their own collective nouns they can look at the ways in which their chosen collective terms suit the nouns concerned.

● **Photocopiable page 19 'Find the collections'**
As already noted, familiarity with examples is a useful way of learning how collective nouns work. Through seeking out the examples and matching them together, children review some of the collective nouns they have already encountered.

Collective noun	Noun
a flock of	birds
a crowd of	people
a bunch of	grapes
a team of	footballers
a swarm of	bees
a herd of	cows
a hand of	bananas
a choir of	singers
a crew of	sailors
a litter of	puppies
a deck of	cards
a school of	whales
a staff of	teachers
a suit of	clothes
a stack of	hay
a pack of	wolves
a forest of	trees
a fleet of	ships

Further ideas

● **Quiz:** Children can make a quiz out of collective nouns and put them to adults to test their knowledge of this aspect of grammar.
● **Collection:** As they read shared texts, listen to people talking and view various media, children can stay on the lookout for other examples of collective nouns.

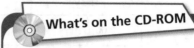

What's on the CD-ROM

On the CD-ROM you will find:
● Printable versions of all three photocopiable pages.
● Answers to 'A pile of guesses' and 'Find the collections'.
● Interactive version of 'A pile of guesses'.

Collective nouns

A pile of guesses

Collective nouns name collections. 'Flock' is a collective noun.

The name of a collection of sheep is a 'flock'.

■ Look at the collective nouns. Cut them out and match them to the things they collect.
■ Compare your results with a friend.

Collective nouns		Nouns	
a flock of	a litter of	trees	clothes
a crowd of	a deck of	singers	sailors
a bunch of	a school of	whales	wolves
a team of	a staff of	ships	cows
a swarm of	a suit of	birds	cards
a herd of	a stack of	bees	bananas
a hand of	a pack of	grapes	teachers
a choir of	a forest of	puppies	people
a crew of	a fleet of	hay	footballers

Illustrations © 1999, Jane Cope.

Name:

Collective nouns

Make up collective nouns

■ Here are some things for which we couldn't find collective nouns! Can you make up collective nouns for them? You might use a word you already know (such as a noise of teachers). You could make one up (such as a moanmoanmoan of teachers). You could use a collective noun you already know (such as a swarm of teachers).

| A _____ | A _____ | A _____ |
| of slugs | of vets | of school dinners |

| A _____ | A _____ | A _____ |
| of smelly socks | of dentists | of monsters |

| A _____ | A _____ | A _____ |
| of fairies | of aliens | of puddles |

■ Choose **four** of your favourite collective nouns from above. Record them in this table. Explain why you chose your collective noun.

Item	Collective noun	Why I chose the collective noun

■ Can you think of other things you could create collective nouns for?

Collective nouns

Find the collections

■ Look at this wordsearch. Try finding **ten** collective nouns. Write them in the table below. Try to find the things they collect. Write these alongside their collective nouns.

Collective noun	Collects	Collective noun	Collects

z	n	o	t	r	e	e	s	g	c	p	n	s	u	c
w	h	l	p	a	b	u	n	c	h	k	r	a	z	a
h	s	c	h	o	o	l	v	o	e	q	j	b	g	r
a	e	s	n	v	d	a	r	w	s	v	h	e	r	d
l	j	c	l	o	t	h	e	s	t	l	a	e	a	s
e	k	r	a	d	c	p	e	o	p	l	e	s	p	c
s	f	o	r	e	s	t	q	f	x	s	m	w	e	g
t	v	w	n	b	m	o	d	r	a	w	e	r	s	f
k	x	d	e	c	k	x	t	e	t	a	b	p	q	x
a	h	i	w	b	i	r	d	s	y	r	s	u	i	t
f	l	o	c	k	a	n	v	z	o	m	n	f	g	z

Person

Objective

Understand the need for grammatical agreement.

Background knowledge

Pronouns and nouns can be used in the first, second or third person. The different types of person are indicated by the use of subject pronouns (such as 'I' and 'she') and verbs.
● **First-person verbs:** identify with the speaker or writer, either alone (*I swam*) or as part of a group (*we swam*).
● **Second-person verbs:** identify with one addressed by the speaker or writer (*You must remember…*).
● **Third-person verbs:** identify with a third party or thing who is neither the one addressing nor the one addressed (*He shouted*, *It fell*).

Activities

In children's language use, the teaching of person should be oriented towards securing grammatical agreement within sentences. Children need to be aware that some verb forms agree according to the person addressed – 'you were', as opposed to 'you was'.
● **Photocopiable page 21 'Choose the right word'**
There are only certain words that will fit the spaces in these sentences. Children will need to read around the spaces looking at other parts of the sentence that give clues to which word should be used. As children try to find the right word to fit the spaces in the sentences, they can try to use a process of elimination. They can look out for the words that do not fit into the spaces and, on this basis, work out which words do.
● **Photocopiable page 22 'Person'**
As children change the person of these sentences they should be encouraged to use the guidance on the photocopiable sheet as a way of figuring out their rewordings. The idea of the sentences pointing can be a helpful way of deciding how to reword sentences in the first, second and third person.
● **Photocopiable page 23 'Person in texts'**
These text extracts show varying examples of person and also introduce the way in which different types of text use this aspect of grammar in different ways. The use of the first-person pronoun and verb is natural in diary writing, as is the use of the second person for instructions in a recipe. This use of person in the structuring of texts is something children will revisit as they attempt to write a wider range of texts.

Further ideas

● **Pass the sentence:** Children can try working in threes to say a sentence in the first person (*I found a sweet*), then pass it on. The next speaker has to say the same thing in the second person pointing to the original speaker (*You found a sweet*). The last speaker has to point to the first and say the same thing in the third person (*She found a sweet*). They can try doing this quickly and helping each other with any difficult examples.
● **Text sorting:** Children can look at different extracts from a range of texts to see what person tends to be used. They can look for correspondences between the job done and the person of a text, such as the use of second person in directions.

What's on the CD-ROM

On the CD-ROM you will find:
● Printable versions of all three photocopiable pages.
● Answers to all three photocopiable pages.
● Interactive versions of 'Choose the right word' and 'Person in texts'.

Person

Choose the right word

■ Look at these sentences.
■ Choose a word from the word box that will fit the space in each sentence.
■ When you have finished, draw a comic strip of the story on the back of this sheet. Use speech bubbles to show what the characters are saying.

Yesterday Mel and Terry _____ climbing a tree.

Mel _____ climbing fastest. Terry _____ a bit slower

but _____ said, "We _____ the best climbers."

Mel waved _____ arms and said, "Look at _____

I _____ better than _____ ."

Terry said, "Don't say that. It _____ a race."

Mel said, "Yes it _____ and I _____winning."

Just then _____ foot slipped. _____ grabbed a

branch.

"Careful! _____ nearly fell," Terry shouted. _____

both started to climb down.

	they	was		she	am
are		you		her	
			her		her
		am		were	
	isn't				
			he		
me				you	was
		is			

Name:

Person

Person

Texts can be written in the first person, the second person or the third person.

First-person words are words that point to the writer.
Words like 'I' 'we' 'my' 'our'.

'I wrote this.'

Second-person words are words that point to the reader.
Words like 'you' and 'your'.

'You should read this.'

Third-person words are words that point to other things or people.
Words like 'he' 'she' 'it' 'them'.

'He is over there.'

■ These sentences are written in the first person. Can you change them to the second person? Can you then change them to the third person?

I kicked the ball. → You kicked the ball. → He kicked the ball.

I played my games. _____

We ate all our biscuits. _____

I read this all by myself. _____

_____

This house is mine. _____

■ Can you try the same changes with **six** sentences you have made up?

Illustrations © 1999, Jane Cope.

Person

Person in texts

■ Look at these snippets of text. Are they written in the first person, second person or third person?

■ Circle the words that tell you which person the text is written in.

■ Can you take a sentence from each text and change the person?

Extract from a recipe
To make an omelette you will need two eggs and some butter.

First you beat the eggs until the white is mixed with the yolk. Then you melt the butter in a frying pan. You may need to ask a grown up to help you with this.

Message from librarian to class 4
Message for class 4: Could you bring your library books when you come to the hall? You will be going straight to the library after assembly. Take your book bags from the basket in the classroom and tick yourself off on the list by the door.

Experiment
The snails were placed in their tank along with lettuce, chocolate and a piece of bread. They were checked after one hour. Three of the snails were eating the lettuce. None of them was eating the chocolate. None of them was eating the bread.

Extract from newspaper article
Carrie Lewis has fulfilled her ambition. She has been chosen to play for England. Carrie, aged 10, received a letter yesterday saying she had been selected for the England under-11 team. Now she is getting herself ready to travel down to London for training.

SCHOLASTIC
www.scholastic.co.uk   PHOTOCOPIABLE   Scholastic Literacy Skills
Grammar and punctuation: Year 3   23

Pronouns take their place

Objective

Substitute pronouns for nouns.

Background knowledge

Pronouns are often used to make sentences more readable. A sentence like *Leah rode Leah's bike to Leah's house* is an oddity. The form *Leah rode her bike to her house* is tidier.

The link between the pronoun and the noun for which it stands is called a 'reference'. There are two types of reference:

● **Cataphoric reference:** is a pronoun that refers to a noun that follows it in a text. For example, *Because he wasn't looking, Sam tripped up*.

● **Anaphoric reference:** is a pronoun that refers to a noun that has already occurred in a text (for example, *Sam said he was tired*). To avoid ambiguity, the pronoun needs clear referential relationship with a noun.

Activities

As children begin to reflect on pronouns, they need to focus on their own use of this type of word. They can begin to check in their own writing for the clarity with which they use pronouns.

● **Photocopiable page 25 'Change the sentence'**
As children substitute pronouns for noun phrases the results will vary. A sentence like *Don't eat the cakes* could be changed to *Don't eat them* or *Don't eat those*. It may be interesting to look at the pronoun children use for *My best friend... Will they use 'he' or 'she'? What guided their choice?

● **Photocopiable page 26 'What do they refer to?'**
This missing word activity works on the referential function of pronouns. To find the appropriate word children will need to consider what the pronouns actually refer to.

● **Photocopiable page 27 'Choose the pronoun'**
As children consider their options for the pronoun they could select for the sentences, there will be discussion. Some of the children may have encountered younger children who would say *Me went to the beach*. In certain dialects *Us teacher* as opposed to *Our teacher* could be used. The various possibilities can provide some insights into the varied uses of pronouns and their commonly accepted usage.

Further ideas

● **Pronoun links:** Children can look for pronouns in a text, such as a newspaper article, and circle examples. In the same text, they can then try to find the noun the pronoun stands in for. They can circle the noun and link it to the pronoun.

● **Reference:** Children can look at the position of pronouns in relation to their nouns. They can see if the pronoun precedes or follows the noun. Obscure though they may be, terms like 'anaphoric' and 'cataphoric' can go down well with children.

What's on the CD-ROM

On the CD-ROM you will find:
● Printable versions of all three photocopiable pages.
● Answers to all three photocopiable pages.
● Interactive versions of 'Change the sentence' and 'Choose the pronoun'.

Pronouns take their place

Change the sentence

■ Look at these sentences. Find one word in the word box that can stand in for the phrase in bold. Change them and write them in the space underneath.

■ List the pronouns you used and the phrases they stood in for.

I saw **the little boy** fall off his skateboard.

I saw him fall off his skateboard.

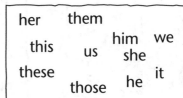

her   them
this   us   him   we
these   she
        those   he   it

Julie played on **her new roller skates**.

_____

Don't eat **the cakes**.

_____

Can Warren play with **the computer games?**

_____

Did you find **the lost key?**

_____

The teacher told **Leila and me** we could use **the cricket bat**.

_____

The boy gave **his little sister** a sweet.

_____

The teacher said, "Give me **the sweets!**"

_____

Mum couldn't get **the television** to work.

_____

Shaun said **Josh and I** could have a go on **his bike**.

_____

My best friend can do a magic trick.

_____

SCHOLASTIC
www.scholastic.co.uk   **PHOTOCOPIABLE**   Scholastic Literacy Skills
Grammar and punctuation: Year 3   **25**

Name:

Pronouns take their place

What do they refer to?

■ Look at the gaps in the sentences below. Find a word in the pronoun box that fits in each gap.

hers	that	mine
we	you
them	him	they
I	us
she	it	he
our	they	himself

The animals were at a party. _____ were bored. Monkey wanted

to cheer _____ up. She found a tree stump and jumped on

_____ .

She shouted to the animals "Hey _____ lot – look at me."

She did a funny dance. _____ bopped and jived. The animals

laughed so loudly _____ gave themselves tummy aches.

The camel was not pleased. _____ was so jealous.

When the monkey was finished he clambered onto the tree stump.

"If she can do it so can _____," he thought. He did a dance.

"I bet _____ is better than _____ ," he said to

_____ .

The animals thought camel was awful. They shouted " _____ is

rubbish. What do you take _____ for? _____ don't want

any old dancing. Bring back _____ friend the monkey."

They sent _____ packing.

Rewritten from Aesop's Fables

PHOTOCOPIABLE   **■SCHOLASTIC**
www.scholastic.co.uk

Pronouns take their place

Choose the pronoun

■ Look at the sentences below. There are three possible pronouns in each one. Rewrite the sentences, choosing the pronoun that suits the sentence.

Give the torch to   my. / me. / I.   _____

Yesterday   my / I / me   went to the beach. _____

He / Him / His   played on the swing. _____

This is   our / we / us   house. _____

We want   us / our / we   playtime. _____

I blew   my / our / mine   nose. _____

He whistled to   he. / himself. / herself. _____

Our teacher lost   he / him / his   keys. _____

My mum let me help   her / she / I   cook the tea. _____

We / Us / Our   teacher told   we / us / our   off. _____

Today   me / I / our   gran is coming to visit. _____

This / These / Those   book is   me. / I. / mine. _____

Writing with nouns and pronouns

Objective

Understand and apply the concept of person in relation to nouns.

Writing focus

Through looking at the use of nouns and pronouns, children tackle the correct use of person in plurals and writing.

Skills to writing

● **Today's plurals**

The children will only grasp the rules for turning singular into plural by continued reinforcement. Over several weeks, write a collection of nouns on a sheet of paper and place them in a location where the children can see them. Invite the children, as they enter the class in the morning or after breaks, to reflect on how they would turn the words into a plural. Periodically, ask the children to make the words plural in writing.

● **Reviewing plurals**

Ask children to look back over completed pieces of writing finding the various plurals they have used. Last year's writing book can provide some good raw material – children enjoy looking back at writing from some time ago, particularly if they can now find and correct their work. As they look through their writing, ask the children to find some singular nouns and check they would know how to write the plural. By doing this, it encourages them to go back to their own writing and review their own vocabulary.

● **Have a go**

When introducing the various ways of forming plurals it is important to ensure children still feel confident enough to have a go at spelling even if they are not sure which ending to use. Explain to the class that a few incorrect plurals can provide good raw material for revision of such spellings. Tell the children you are going to keep a list of different plurals used over the course of the week's writing. Which rule do the children expect to be the most common? Which turns out to be the most common?

● **Report text nouns**

Nouns can provide a useful means of planning and structuring report texts. A good first step to writing a report text can be to think of the 'nouns within the noun'. For example, take a subject, such as 'The playground', the children can make a list of all the nouns associated with it, for example the football pitch, a climbing frame and so on. Using 'a' or 'the' before each will help the children to check they are using the right sort of word. The children can then use the list, putting it into a logical order, and fleshing it out to create their report.

● **Person and text type**

It is important to work on person with the children to ensure the consistency of their writing. It is not uncommon for children to switch person halfway through a piece of work. A good way of doing this is to explore some of the text types which children are asked to write. A personal recount, such as a diary entry, will use the first person. A report text will be written in the third person. Persuasive texts can be written in the second person (*You should recycle newspaper because…*).

Activities

● **Photocopiable page 30 'Report planner'**

This particular writing frame focuses on the use of nouns in report writing. It asks children to think of the subject for their report and to think of three sub-divisions for the subject matter. Once they have done this they are asked to sub-divide each section into a further two or three nouns. For example, if they are writing about their family they may choose 'mum, gran, brother' as the three initial nouns. The next step is the more challenging. Can they think of two or three nouns about which they have something more to say? If Gran lives in a great big house they may note 'house' in one of her spaces.

● **Photocopiable page 31 'Missing words'**

In each of the sentences on the photocopiable sheet there are a range of nouns that could be used to fill the spaces. Children can work in twos and threes to come up with a list of possibilities for each of the spaces. They can then think about how some of their chosen alternatives could be used in a short story idea they plan together.

Write on

● **The fairy and the tomato**

Work backwards from the various types of plural to generate some strange story or poetry ideas. Firstly list the rules for making nouns plural. Then ask the children to think of one noun that follows each of the rules and use the four nouns they come up with in a brief story of their own devising. What, for example, could the story of 'The Fairy and the Tomato' conjure up?

● **The…climbed**

Provide the children with a range of sentences where the noun is missing. Ask the children to look at the sentence and see if they can come up with a range of possible words to fill the gap. If, for example, the sentence is *The…climbed the tree*, the missing word could be feasible ('girl', 'koala') or more outlandish ('alien', 'teacher').

● **'It' bit more**

When revising writing, ask children to try a pronoun addition on some of the sentences they have already written. This can provide a way of extending writing to provide more feeling or extended detail. For example, if they have written, *The sun shelter is on the playground*, can they think which pronoun they would use for an extra fact. In the sun shelter's case they would use 'it', so they should think of a sentence that starts *It…* which could add a bit of extra thought or detail to their writing: *The sun shelter is on the playground. It is bright green.*

● **Revising writing**

Stop as you are reading or writing and revisit some of the nouns, checking whether they are single or plural, and that children could change from one to the other by applying the correct rule.

● **Nonsense nouns**

Nonsense noun poems can provide a great way of generating play with word sounds. The task involves inventing new nouns – and keeping all verbs and adjectives conventional. Children then write an expressive poem about the strange noun of their creation, adding in new nouns as they go along:

The scrumbly has got long dleeeps
and a glibble made of splee

Of course, the great thing is they are so easy to rhyme – but that's where 'Jabberwocky' came from!

What's on the CD-ROM

On the CD-ROM you will find:
● Printable versions of both photocopiable pages.

Name:

Report planner

- Think of a subject and write in the box on the left.
- Then think of three nouns to describe it and write those in the middle three boxes.
- Write three nouns to describe those and write them on the three lines.

1.

2.

3.

1.

2.

3.

1.

2.

3.

Writing with nouns and pronouns

Missing words

■   Collect a list of words which could fit in the sentences below. Write them in the appropriate boxes.

■   Choose the best words and write the complete sentences on the lines below.

The [   ] fell off the [   ] .

The [   ] found a [   ] .

The [   ] escaped from a [   ] .

The [   ] was chased by a [   ] .

The [   ] discovered a secret [   ] .

The noisy [   ] disturbed the [   ] .

Silently, we entered the [   ] .

"Look out, it's a [   ] ."

_____

_____

_____

_____

_____

Pronouns

Introduction

Children understand pronouns better when they understand the role they perform in substituting for nouns. In this chapter, activities include looking at different types of pronoun and how they develop clarity and cohesion in writing. Throughout there is an emphasis on exploring these grammatical features in real contexts – such as comics and conversations.

Poster notes

The pronouns (page 33)
This poster presents the various words that can function as personal pronouns. They are organised into rows of singular and plural pronouns. Children may note the way in which some pronouns retain a particular form within a variety of columns. The poster provides an opportunity for children to think of sentences in which they would use particular pronouns.

Person (page 34)
The same pronouns are organised into the first, second and third person. Children could try figuring out which ones are singular and which are plural.

In this chapter

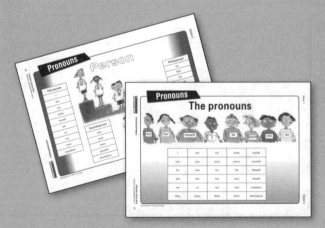

Pronouns

The pronouns

I	me		my	mine	myself
you	you		your	yours	yourself
he	him		his	his	himself
she	her		her	hers	herself
we	us		our	ours	ourselves
they	them		their	theirs	themselves

Pronouns

Person

Third person
he
him
his
himself
she
her
hers
herself
they
them
their
theirs
themselves

Second person
you
your
yours
yourself
yourselves

First person
I
me
my
mine
myself
we
us
our
ours
ourselves

Illustrations © 2008, Jane Cope.

PHOTOCOPIABLE

Pronouns

Objective

Identify pronouns.

Background knowledge

Pronouns are words that are substituted for nouns or noun phrases. In the sentence *Joe gave the cake to Samia* the noun 'Joe' can be substituted for the pronoun 'he' to make *He gave the cake to Samia*. The other nouns, 'the cake' and 'Samia', can also be substituted to make *He gave it to her*.

Pronouns are relatively anonymous words. In the above example 'Joe' may be a particular person but 'He' could refer to any one of half the population. Similarly 'the cake' is more definite than 'it'. When pronouns are used they tend to require a shared understanding of whom or what they refer to.

Pronouns stand in for nouns but, unlike nouns, they cannot be modified by adjectives. So whereas the usage *He gave the delicious cake to her* is straightforward, the sentence *He gave the delicious it to her* isn't. The only way of using an adjective here would be to use the construction *the…one*, as in *the delicious one* – but this implies a further meaning that there is 'one' that *isn't* delicious.

Activities

Children need to understand a pronoun is one of a relatively small family of words that can be substituted for a noun. Once they have seen a list of the words that can perform this function (see photocopiable page 36 'Who is "you"?'), they will often begin to find examples in texts they read.

● **Photocopiable page 36 'Who is "you"?'**
This activity takes children through a text artificially inflated with pronouns. This gives children an idea of the way such words function. One way of reading the text is for children to imagine the pronouns as words that are pointing and, as they read them, to ask *Who am I pointing at as I say this word?* The idea of pointing as they say 'we' or 'that' should enhance the way the pronouns work in this text.

● **Photocopiable page 37 'Pronouns in action'**
As children undertake this activity they need a variety of texts. You may find it useful to skim read the texts beforehand to check which pronouns they contain. Children may also use texts they bring from home in which they have noticed pronouns.

● **Photocopiable page 38 'Awkward sentences'**
As children read the sentences in this activity they are asked to alter the ones that sound 'awkward'. This may provide an opportunity to discuss the redrafting or editing process that takes place in the production of texts and ask children to imagine they are undertaking this task.

Further ideas

● **Exhaustive list:** The pronoun family is not vast. Children may be able to compile the exhaustive list. As they read through various texts they can put forward examples they find of words that may be pronouns. The class can consider whether or not they are and, if so, add them to the list.

● **Newspaper circling:** Children can work in threes and fours looking through a copy of a newspaper and circling all the words they think may be pronouns. They may be able to handle the task of applying the question: *If this word is a pronoun, what noun does it stand for?*

● **Customise 'you':** Once they have tried photocopiable page 36 'Who is "you"?', children can try to produce their own example using a text. They can isolate the pronouns and write, in the margins, the questions the reader needs to answer in order to understand the pronoun being used.

What's on the CD-ROM

On the CD-ROM you will find:
● Printable versions of all three photocopiable pages.
● Answers to 'Who is "you"?' and 'Awkward sentences'.
● Interactive version of 'Awkward sentences'.

Name:

Pronouns

Who is 'you'?

■ Look at the story below. It includes the following pronouns:

you	their	that	those	they
us	them	him	our	it
he	yourself	she	we	

■ These pronouns refer to someone or something. They stand in for a noun (the name of something).

■ Who or what does each of the pronouns in the story refer to? The pronouns are the words shown in bold type. Write the noun referred to above each pronoun.

Monty and Natasha's walk

Natasha took Monty her dog for **their** afternoon walk.

He didn't like being on **his** lead so he pulled and pulled at it. Natasha let **him**

lead the way. As they walked **she** chatted to herself.

"Where are **you** taking **us**?" she asked Monty.

They came to the park.

"We can stop here if you like," she said. "**We** don't need to be home for **our**

tea yet."

She found a stick and threw **it**.

"Can you chase **that**?" she said. Monty found it.

Then she threw two sticks. "OK" she shouted, "Chase **those**."

She threw **them** as far as she could. **They** landed up in a tree!

"Fetch them **yourself**," Monty growled.

Pronouns

Pronouns in action

■　Gather together a range of texts. You could look in picture books, a newspaper, an advert, a letter… any texts you choose.

■　Look in each of your texts for the pronouns below. When you find an example fill in the chart below.

I　me　my　mine　myself　you　yours　yourself　he　him　his　himself　she her　hers　herself　we　us　our　ours　ourselves　they　them their　theirs　it　its　itself　this　these　that　those

■　Write the pronouns in the pronoun column below.
■　Next to the pronoun write the person or thing it stands in for.

Pronouns	What the pronoun stands in for (the noun)

Name:

Pronouns

Awkward sentences

■ Some of the nouns in these sentences don't need to be there.

> Dave found (Dave's) coat.

They could be taken away: | Dave found (Dave's) coat.

and pronouns could be put in their place: | Dave found his coat.

■ Replace the circled nouns with pronouns. Write them above each of the circled words.

> his   it   her   I   she   him   us
> them   they   his   our   me
> he   you   my   we   their

After school

Dave forgot (Dave's) coat.

Carrie bought an apple and ate (the apple).

Carrie asked (Carrie's) mum, "Can (Carrie) have an ice cream?"

Mel got (Mel's) football then (Mel) went out to play.

Dave's teacher told (Dave) that (Dave) had forgotten (Dave's) coat.

Mel told Carrie, "(Carrie) can borrow (Mel's) pencil."

Joe and Rose asked (Joe and Rose's) mum, "Can (Joe and Rose) play outside?"

Joe and Rose told Carrie, "(Carrie) can play with (Joe and Rose) at

(Joe and Rose's) house."

Rose stood on (Rose's) head and said, "Look at (Rose)."

Frank called for Joe and Rose and (Frank) asked (Joe and Rose) if

(Joe and Rose) wanted to play at (Frank's) house.

Illustrations © 1999, Jane Cope.

PHOTOCOPIABLE   ■SCHOLASTIC
www.scholastic.co.uk

Two types of pronoun

Distinguish personal and possessive pronouns.

Background knowledge

There are two types of pronoun.
● **Personal pronouns:** replace the names of people or things, for example 'I', 'me', 'they'.
● **Possessive pronouns:** indicate possession of something, such as 'mine', 'his', 'theirs'. They refer to something in the same context as the pronoun that can be identified as a possession. In the sentence *John took my book*, the use of a possessive pronoun would result in *John took mine*.

Note that the possessive words used attributively (that is to say, *before* the noun), are possessive adjectives, or possessive determiners, since they modify the noun. This category includes words such as 'my', 'your', 'his', 'her' and so on.

Activities

The distinction made between these types of pronoun can provide a way of expanding children's awareness of the pronouns they encounter. It provides two separate ways of thinking about, and looking for, pronouns. Where a possessive pronoun is used they will usually be able to identify the thing that is possessed.
● **Photocopiable page 40 'Two types of pronoun'**
As an introduction to the distinction between personal and possessive pronouns, this activity uses simple sentences and asks children to categorise the pronouns within them.

● **Photocopiable page 41 'Matching personal and possessive'**
The mixing of personal and possessive pronouns in this activity leads children to try matching up sentences in which the two types of pronoun correspond. The emphasis in this activity should be on children saying the sentences aloud to see if the result sounds right.
● **Photocopiable page 42 'Possessives'**
Through reflecting on the different people referred to in this activity, children should fall back on the possessive pronouns and adjectives they know to find the right word to begin each of the sentences. Again, the gender of the person will decide the correct pronoun.

Further ideas

● **Possessive listings:** Using photocopiable page 42 'Possessives' as a starting point, children can write short paragraphs about people, including individuals and groups. They could draw on themselves, their group of friends, a brother or sister as a starting point. Once they have chosen their person or persons they write a few sentences about them, using the appropriate pronouns.
● **Matching:** Children can write the name of a person or group of people on one card and a sentence about them on another. In the sentence they can try using a personal or possessive pronoun. They can then try producing two different cards, choosing whoever they wish provided their choice leads them to use different pronouns.

What's on the CD-ROM

On the CD-ROM you will find:
● Printable versions of all three photocopiable pages.
● Answers to 'Two types of pronoun' and 'Matching personal and possessive'.
● Interactive versions of 'Two types of pronoun' and 'Matching personal and possessive'.

Name:

Two types of pronoun

Two types of pronoun

There are different types of pronoun. The two main types are:

personal pronouns:
pronouns that stand in place of a person or thing ('me', 'I', 'you', 'it')

and

possessive pronouns:
pronouns that show someone owns something ('mine', 'yours', 'ours').

■ Look at the sentences below. Sort them into two groups:
- sentences with personal pronouns
- sentences with possessive pronouns.

Sam is his friend.

I like sweets.

Sian found her shoe.

You are reading.

He fell in the puddle.

The red pencil is mine.

We can go to the park.

Joe took her book.

They are going on holiday.

We can go out to play.

These sweets are all yours.

Our teacher is loud.

Illustrations © 1999, Jane Cope.

Two types of pronoun

Matching personal and possessive

■ Cut out the sentences below.

■ Try matching the sentences on one side of the page with the ones on the other side of the page. The result will be two sentences that fit together.

■ Stick the matching sentences on a separate sheet of paper.

This bike belongs to me.	They are theirs.
This book belongs to you.	It is his.
That coat belongs to him.	They are hers.
This football belongs to her.	They are ours.
This house belongs to them.	They are mine.
This television belongs to us.	They are his.
These stickers belong to me.	It is hers.
These crayons belong to you.	It is ours.
These sandwiches belong to him.	It is yours.
These shoes belong to her.	It is mine.
These sweets belong to them.	They are yours.
These flowers belong to us.	It is theirs.

Name:

Possessives

■ Look at the sentences below. Think about the people referred to in each sentence. Complete the sentence, filling in the possessive pronoun and the end of the sentence.

■ Try some possessive sentences of your own about other people. It could be people in your family or people in your street.

About me. My **task** is finding missing words.	**About my friend.** _____ name is _____ _____
About my school. _____ classrooms are _____ _____	**About our teachers.** _____ staff room is _____ _____
About me and my friend. _____ favourite game is _____ _____	**About my bedroom.** _____ floor is _____ _____
About our headteacher. _____ favourite day of the week is _____ _____	**About me.** _____ favourite pop song is _____ _____

PHOTOCOPIABLE ■SCHOLASTI
www.scholastic.co.u

Different types of pronoun

Objective

Distinguish first-, second- and third-person pronouns.

Background knowledge

Pronouns can be written in the first, second or third person.
● **First-person pronouns:** identify with the speaker or writer, either alone (*I swam*) or as part of a group (*we swam*).
● **Second-person pronouns:** identify with one addressed by the speaking or writing (*You must remember…*).
● **Third-person pronouns:** identify with a third party or thing who is neither the one addressing nor the one addressed (*He shouted*, *It fell*).

Activities

An understanding of first, second and third person can be an important factor in children's writing development. As children work on the style and language of non-fiction texts, they can look at the way certain texts are couched in the first, second or third person. A persuasive text may use the second person (*You should buy this…*) whereas a recount of a personal experience will adopt the first person (*I went to school and I…*).
● **Photocopiable page 44 'Person'**
As with the understanding of what a pronoun stands in for, the initial approach to person can be assisted by pointing. As they read the sentences in this activity the children can imagine themselves saying them to another person (the second person) and pointing at the person to whom the pronoun refers. If they point to themselves the sentence uses the first person. If they point to the listener it uses the second. If they point outside the conversation, the pronoun is in the third person.

● **Photocopiable page 45 'Ways of looking at pronouns'**
Once they have applied the two criteria to the examples on the photocopiable sheet, children could try this activity using other sentences from various texts.
● **Photocopiable page 46 'Pronouns at play'**
This reading activity may be used in shared or guided reading. Once children have read through the script, they should try looking at the various types of pronoun used in the text.

Further ideas

● **Taping:** Children could tape classroom conversation. They could then listen to the tape and consider whether the pronouns used are first, second or third person. They could keep a tally of the most common usage in the conversation.
● **I, you, he texts:** Children could try writing sentences in each person. Once they have completed a set of examples they could look at them to see what text they could imagine such sentences featuring in. What text, for example, would be couched in the second person?

What's on the CD-ROM

On the CD-ROM you will find:
● Printable versions of all three photocopiable pages.
● Answers to 'Person' and 'Ways of looking at pronouns'.
● Interactive versions of 'Person' and 'Ways of looking at pronouns'.

Name:

Different types of pronoun

Person

First-person words	Words that refer to the writer.	How you write if you are writing about yourself.
Second-person words	Words that refer to the reader.	How you write if you are writing about your reader.
Third-person words	Words that refer to other things or people.	How you write if you are writing about someone or something else.

■ Cut out these sentences and say them aloud.

■ Sort them into sentences written in the first person, the second person and the third person. Stick them in their three groups on a separate sheet of paper.

✂

Six o'clock is time for them to have their tea.	They went shopping.	You found the pencil.
We went shopping.	At playtime you saw your sister.	You went shopping.
Six o'clock is time for you to have your tea.	They had chips for their tea.	Six o'clock is time for me to have my tea.
At playtime he saw his sister.	Did you finish the story?	At playtime I saw my sister.
Did he finish the story?	They found the pencil.	You ate all your dinner.
The bike is mine.	I ate all my dinner.	The bike is hers.
Did we finish the story?	The bike is yours.	I had chips for tea.
She ate all her dinner.	You had chips for tea.	We found the pencil.

PHOTOCOPIABLE

Different types of pronoun

Ways of looking at pronouns

- Look at the pronouns used in each of the speech bubbles below.
- Are they personal pronouns or possessive pronouns? Are they first-person, second-person or third-person pronouns? Circle your answers.

I switched on the television.

Personal or possessive?

First person, second person or third person?

My mum likes chocolate.

Personal or possessive?

First person, second person or third person?

Our classroom is tidy.

Personal or possessive?

First person, second person or third person?

Rafi played on his skateboard.

Personal or possessive?

First person, second person or third person?

My sister tidied her room.

Personal or possessive?

First person, second person or third person?

You are smiling.

Personal or possessive?

First person, second person or third person?

Your shirt is ripped.

Personal or possessive?

First person, second person or third person?

The children sang their song.

Personal or possessive?

First person, second person or third person?

Name:

Different types of pronoun

Pronouns at play

- Act out this play with some friends.
- Look at some of the pronouns in the play. Read the play again. Each time you come to a pronoun, stop and point to the character it refers to.

The Tortoise and the Hare

Cast:
Hare, Tortoise, Fox

Fox:　　This is a story of two animals and how they decided who was the fastest.

(Hare is sitting with Fox. Tortoise comes past.)

Hare:　　Hello Tortoise.

Tortoise:　Hello Hare. Hello Fox.

Hare:　　Oh dear, you are so slow.

Tortoise:　Am I?

Hare:　　She is, isn't she, Fox?

Fox:　　Leave her alone, Hare.

Tortoise:　OK Why don't we have a race? The winner will get a medal.

Hare:　　A race! With you! Ha! I will easily win.

Tortoise:　We shall see. Fox, could you start us off?

Fox:　　Alright. Are you ready? Steady? Go?

(Hare runs far into the lead.)

Hare:　　Look at me go. The medal will be mine!

Fox:　　Hurry up Tortoise. Oh dear, she is sure to lose.

Tortoise:　Don't worry about me. I know what I'm doing.

(Hare is well in the lead.)

Hare:　　Where is she? I can't even see her. I think I'll have a rest.

(Falls asleep. Tortoise comes past.)

Tortoise:　Just as I thought. He is fast asleep. Shhh, don't want to wake him.

(Fox stands at the finishing line.)

Fox:　　Come on tortoise. This is your chance to win.

(Hare wakes up. Sees Tortoise crossing line.)

Hare:　　She beat me!

Illustrations © 1999, Jane Cope.

Pronouns in texts

Objective

Investigate the use of pronouns.

Background knowledge

Pronouns can be ambiguous words. For example, a note sent by a member of the public to the local council read: *Our kitchen floor is very damp. We have two children and would like a third. Could you please send someone round to do something about it?* That final 'it' is full of ambiguity.

The clear use of pronouns is a stylistic feature that needs to be considered. Yet the ambiguity can be used to full effect, whether it be in the Thomas Hardy poem on photocopiable page 48 or in a joke like the one used throughout the film *Airplane*:

- Passenger: Hostess, take me to the cockpit!
- Hostess: What is it?
- Passenger: It's a little room at the front of the plane with controls and things, but that's not important right now.

Activities

Through these activities children should grasp the potential in investigating the use of the pronoun. They should also get some idea of the poetic use of this type of word as well as its common use in conversation.

- **Photocopiable page 48 'Waiting Both'**
This activity draws out the poetic use of pronouns to their full effect. As children read the poem they can consider the effect of the use of pronouns as opposed to more specific names.

- **Photocopiable page 49 'Comic pronouns'**
As with many comic stories children will find as they read this text that an understanding of the pronouns depends on an appreciation of what they are referring to. In some cases this will rely on the picture rather than the text. So the 'there' in *Can we go in there?* is only understood through reference to the illustration.
- **Photocopiable page 50 'Pronoun talk'**
As children record and investigate their use of pronouns they can compare their findings with others in the class. They could also swap tapes and listen to the conversations others have taped.

Further ideas

- **Poetry:** Other poems, such as Stevie Smith's 'Not Waving but Drowning' feature consciously ambiguous uses of pronouns. Children could try their own examples.
- **Eerie openings:** Stories can often use pronouns to provide an eerie opening, for example, *He was late. He ran through the streets. What if they got there before him?* Children could try creating their own mysterious story openings in the same vein.

What's on the CD-ROM

On the CD-ROM you will find:
- Printable versions of all three photocopiable pages.
- Answers to 'Comic pronouns'.

Name:

Pronouns in texts

'Waiting Both'

A star looks down at me,
And says: 'Here I am and you
Stand each in our degree:
What do you mean to do,–
  Mean to do?'

I say: 'For all I know,
Wait, and let Time go by
Till my change comes.'–'Just so',
The Star says: 'So mean I:–
  So mean I.'

Thomas Hardy

■ Circle the pronouns in the poem.

■ Look at the words taken from the poem in the boxes below. What do you think about these lines?

A star looks down at me,	I think...

'Here I am and you Stand each in our degree:	I think...

What do you mean to do, – Mean to do?'	I think...

'Wait, and let Time go by Till my change comes.'	I think...

The Star says: 'So mean I:– So mean I.'	I think...

PHOTOCOPIABLE

■SCHOLASTIC
www.scholastic.co.uk

Illustrations © 1999, Jane Cope.

Pronouns in texts

Comic pronouns

■ Read this story. Find the pronouns and circle them.

GRANNY GRAMMAR & THE HAIRCUT

You need a haircut.

This sounds bad.

Can we go in here?

Yoinks! They all look scruffy.

MR BASINS

He will be right for us.

Yikes! My poor hair!

Is he yours?

He's my grandson. Give him a smart cut.

She can't make me!

Get him!

It's them!

He's locked in the cupboard.

Get out of my broom cupboard!

That is what I need!

OK please yourself.

That is nice.

I've got news for you!

You cropped a mop! See ya!

Illustrations © 1999, Jane Cope.

■ Look back at the pronouns. Which person or thing did they refer to?

Name:

Pronouns in texts

Pronoun talk

■ Tape a five-minute conversation with two friends on this subject: 'Things people do at playtime'.

■ Listen to the recording. Write down some of the pronouns used in the discussion in the speech box. In the tag alongside, record what or whom the pronouns referred to.

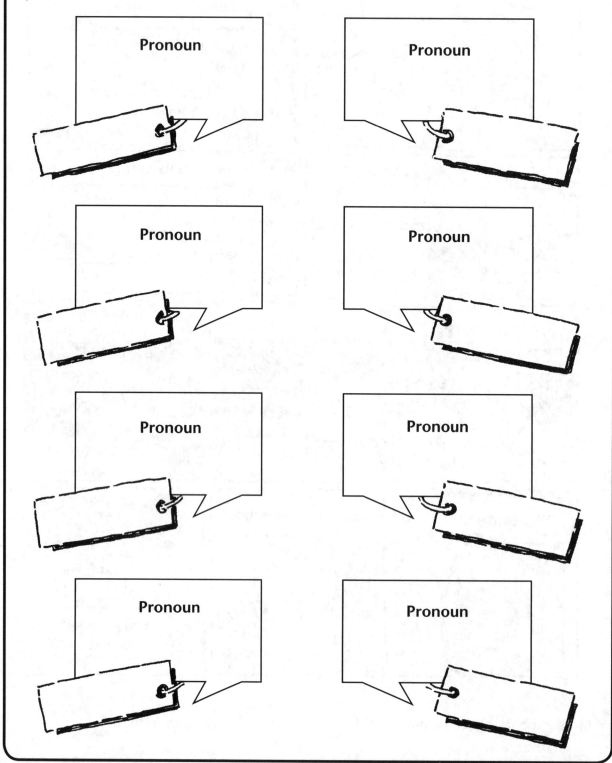

PHOTOCOPIABLE

Pronouns in writing

Objective

Extend the use of pronouns in writing.

Writing focus

Building on the previous activities on nouns and pronouns, this section revisits the different types of pronoun children will use in their writing.

Skills to writing

● **Meet the family**
The pronoun family isn't the biggest of crowds (many of them being represented on poster page 33 'The pronouns') but children's accurate grasp of their use and spelling provides a vital toolkit for writing. During shared reading and writing, stop occasionally to check a pronoun and look at what sort it is and what it refers to.

● **Reference**
A feature of pronoun use to explore with the children in their writing is the clarity of reference. The activities in this chapter will present a few examples of sentences where it isn't crystal clear what the pronouns are referring to. If children write *He saw it*, encourage them to check that their reader will know who 'he' was and what 'it' is.

● **Cohesion**
Reference is one of the ways in which writers hold their texts together. It can be seen in this very sentence, where the opening 'it' made a link between this sentence and the word 'reference' earlier in the paragraph. As children reach the junior years and their writing grows from sentences to a number of paragraphs, the knitting together of the text can be reinforced through ensuring pronouns are used with clarity.

● **Second person**
Watch out for some of the interesting contexts in which the second person is used. Classic examples include the opening lines of the television series 'The Twilight Zone' in which we were told, *You are travelling on a journey*. Other interesting examples include the use of the second person in persuasive advertising (*You want the best for your hair*) and adventure-game stories (*You land on a strange island. You have to choose one of two pathways*).

● **Playscripts and drama**
As was demonstrated on photocopiable page 46 'Pronouns at play', the use of pronouns in playscripts and drama provides an interesting opportunity to check that the reader and user of the script is clear about what is being referred to. During drama activities, children can think of lines and instances where it needs to be clear who is referring to what. If, in a piece of drama, someone is saying *Bring it here*, they can explore what 'it' is, and why it needs to be 'here'.

Activities

● **Photocopiable page 53 'Autobiography planner'**
As part of their work on the first person children can devise a recount text that consists of their first person memories. Using the planner they can construct a set of ideas for a recount of their own life story. When they are writing this encourage them to think of their own 'I' and 'we' memories, but also to look at the involvement of other people in their experiences – 'he', 'she' and 'they'.

● **Photocopiable page 54 'Instruction frame'**
Instructional texts provide examples of the use of the second-person pronoun directing the reader as to what 'you' need to do. While some use the imperative verb and just order the reader to *Take a tomato and slice it*, others use the form presented in this writing frame – *First you…* When using the frame children won't necessarily use each of the 'you' lines, but the spaces in the photocopiable can be cut out or more can be added in to provide clear instructions to 'you the reader'. This can be used to support the application of the second person pronoun to children's writing of instructions.

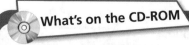

Write on

● **Pronoun sentences**

Encourage children to try devising sentences with loads of pronouns in them. It doesn't matter what story they are telling – the purpose is to gather an array of pronouns and allow them to stretch out the sentence. For example: *He saw me dropping these so he picked them up and gave them to you.* Once they have devised an elongated sentence they like, children can illustrate it, possibly giving some insight into what the sentence was all about.

● **Opening ambiguity**

While it's vital to ensure clear reference in the use of pronouns, a bit of ambiguity can be used to good effect. Opening lines like: *He sat bolt upright* or *'What was that?' she whispered*, act as hooks to a reader. We want to know who 'he' is, what's going on and what 'that' was. In their narrative writing, children can be encouraged to open a story or a chapter with an ambiguous pronoun that will make the reader want to know to what the pronouns refer.

● **What is that?**

Using the endings on photocopiable page 41 'Matching personal and possessive', children can devise their own first sentences that would fit the various endings. Starting with *It is hers*, can they think of a sentence that could precede this – such as *The rabbit belongs to the girl, The girl has a pink rabbit.* They can explore different ways of shaping sentences to match the pronoun example.

● **Comic pronouns**

Children can produce their own comic stories, similar to *Granny grammar* (see photocopiable page 49 'Comic pronouns'). As they do this, encourage them to use pronouns, as we would in everyday speech – *Catch these! Look at him!* In doing so they need to make sure that it is clear from the illustrations – the way the characters point, move and look – what the pronoun refers to.

What's on the CD-ROM

On the CD-ROM you will find:
● Printable versions of both photocopiable pages.

Pronouns in writing

Autobiography planner

■ Use this planner to make notes and plan a recount of your own life story.
■ Remember to think of:
  • the events that will interest the readers
  • the characters who appeared in your story
  • things people said at the time.

Being born	My family
When I was very little	My first memories
Favourite day out	First day at school
Meeting someone special	Making friends

Illustrations © 1999, Jane Cope.

Name:

Pronouns in writing

Instruction frame

■ Use this frame to write the instructions your readers should follow to carry out a task.

To…
You will need…
First you…
Then you…
Next you…
Then you…
Finally you…

Chapter 3

Adjectives

Introduction

The focus of this chapter is on the introduction and exploration of adjectives in real contexts. For this reason there is a two-fold emphasis on exploring texts and developing children's own creative use of this word class. The writing activities at the end focus on children seeking opportunities for their use in persuasive writing. There is also a clear request to gather loads of good and well-used examples of adjectives for writing.

Poster notes

Adjectives (page 56)
The poster provides a list of various types of adjectives, and can be used as a way of introducing adjectives, as well as in activities in which children use or classify various adjectives.

The Listeners (page 57)
The poem 'The Listeners', by Walter de la Mare, features in the 'Find the adjective in…' activity on page 62. The full text is reprinted here. The poem contains a mysterious text that children will be able to follow, but one that is rich with interesting and poetic adjectives.

In this chapter

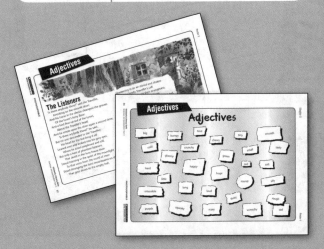

Adjectives

SCHOLASTIC
www.scholastic.co.uk

Adjectives

The Listeners

'Is there anybody there?' said the Traveller,
  Knocking on the moonlit door;
And his horse in the silence champed the grasses
  Of the forest's ferny floor:
And a bird flew up out of the turret,
  Above the Traveller's head:
And he smote upon the door again a second time;
  'Is there anybody there?' he said.
But no one descended to the Traveller;
  No head for the leaf-fring'd sill
Leaned over and looked into his grey eyes,
  Where he stood perplexed and still.
But only a host of phantom listeners
  That dwelt in the lone house then
Stood listening in the quiet of the moonlight
  To that voice from the world of men:
Stood thronging the faint moonbeams on the dark stair,
  That goes down to the empty hall,

Hearkening in an air stirred and shaken
  By the lonely Traveller's call.
And he felt in his heart their strangeness,
  Their stillness answering his cry,
While his horse moved, cropping the dark turf,
  'Neath the starred and leafy sky;
For he suddenly smote on the door, even
  Louder, and lifted his head: –
'Tell them I came, and no one answered,
  That I kept my word,' he said.
Never the least stir made the listeners,
  Though every word he spake
Fell echoing through the shadowiness of the still house
  From the one man left awake:
Ay, they heard his foot upon the stirrup,
  And the sound of iron on stone,
And how the silence surged slowly backward,
  When the plunging hoofs were gone.

Walter de la Mare

Text © 1912, Walter de la Mare. Illustrations © 2008, Jane Cope.

What is an adjective?

Objective

Define the function of adjectives.

Background knowledge

Adjectives describe or modify nouns. In sentences like *The big dog chased me* and *Today is a sunny day*, the words 'big' and 'sunny' modify the noun. Adjectives can occur in two places:

● **Attributive adjectives:** come before a noun (*The red* book).
● **Predicative adjectives:** come after a noun (*The dog is* **fierce**).

Most adjectives can be both attributive or predicative, depending upon the context. However, an adjective like 'mere' is only used in an attributive way, whereas an adjective like 'abroad' is only used in a predicative way.

Activities

For children with a developing vocabulary, adjectives are something of an extra to the sense of sentences. They could get by with *The dog chased me*. However, teachers should be striving to develop the children's use of language to include the elaboration to create sentences like *The big dog chased me*.

● **Photocopiable page 59 'Using adjectives'**
As an initial activity, this photocopiable sheet asks children to think of words they would use to describe the nouns shown. Once they have completed these, it may be interesting to compare their results to see whether any common adjectives have been applied to particular nouns.

● **Photocopiable page 60 'Qualifying the noun'**
In this activity, children look at the illustrations and try to think of a word they would use to describe the noun shown in the illustration. You may wish to enlarge the sheet to provide more writing space.

● **Photocopiable page 61 'Adjectives in texts'**
To undertake this activity, children will need to be equipped with a range of texts that they can cut up, such as newspapers, leaflets and so on. This activity sets them off on a search for different adjectives.

Further ideas

● **Collecting:** Once they have been introduced to adjectives, children can start a collection of various examples. These can be recorded along with the noun that each one modifies.
● **Shared reading:** During shared reading activities, children can look out for adjectives. The discovery of new adjectives needs to be coupled with looking for the noun they modify.

What's on the CD-ROM

On the CD-ROM you will find:
● Printable versions of all three photocopiable pages.

What is an adjective?

Using adjectives

■ Invent some story characters. Draw them in the spaces below and write some words that describe them. Is your monster scary or sensible?

Devise a monster...   Devise a robot...

_____   _____

_____   _____

_____   _____

_____   _____

Devise a dragon...   Devise a wizard...

_____   _____

_____   _____

_____   _____

_____   _____

Name:

What is an adjective?

Qualifying the noun

■ Look at the pictures and text below. Think of a word that could tell us what the object is like, for example, the *thin* hand, the *slender* hand.

the _____ hand

the _____ monster

the _____ spaceship

the _____ day

the _____ star

the _____ cat

the _____ ring

the _____ dog

the _____ fire

the _____ mug

the _____ house

the _____ ball

the _____ pirate

the _____ bath

the _____ bird

the _____ snake

the _____ mouse

the _____ music

the _____ baby

the _____ dress

the _____ elephant

Illustrations © 1999, Jane Cope.

PHOTOCOPIABLE

What is an adjective?

Adjectives in text

■ Collect some examples of sentences with adjectives. Stick or copy them into the sentence column in the table. What are the adjectives describing? What description are they making?

Sentence	What is being described?	How is it described?
This charming house is situated on a quiet street.	the house the street	charming quiet

Identifying adjectives

Identify adjectives.

Background knowledge

One of the main ways in which adjectives can be identified is to look for the nouns that they modify.

Adjectives describe nouns and, while they may come in an attributive or predicative position, the understanding of adjectives is usually dependent upon an awareness of the noun they are modifying.

Words that are not usually thought of as adjectives can perform an adjectival function, so a word like 'sitting', while usually seen as a verb, can be used in a context like *a sitting duck* or *sitting tenant* to modify a noun.

Activities

The identification of adjectives is something that has to be taught in conjunction with the function of adjectives (see 'What is an adjective' on page 58). The aim of this section is that children look at words that are modifying nouns. The term 'modify' may or may not be used in the classroom but the idea should underpin work on this aspect of grammar.

● **Photocopiable page 63 'Find the adjective in...'**
As a stimulus to this activity, children can look at texts and follow the work on photocopiable page 61 'Adjectives in texts'. They can look through the texts printed here for examples of adjectives and look beyond these to other texts.

● **Photocopiable page 64 'Descriptive spaces'**
This activity works on the type of changes adjectives make in a sentence. Each of the sentences works well on its own but can be added to by inserting adjectives. Children can begin to understand where adjectives get placed and the sorts of changes they make.

● **Photocopiable page 65 'Adjectives in poems'**
Poetry can provide a rich resource for finding the uses of adjectives. The examples shown should act as a starting point from which children can explore other examples.

Further ideas

● **Fields of adjectives:** Children can collect similar leaflets and promotional material such as estate agent leaflets, holiday brochures and prize-draw junk mail. The main thing is to begin with publications that have a common thread. They can look through these and see which adjectives commonly appear in these materials.

● **Adjectives in pictures:** Looking at pictures, whether they be photos from magazines or paintings in a gallery, children can look at items in the picture and think of the adjective they would use to describe them. They need to name something or someone in the picture and decide on an adjective that describes the noun.

● **Selling properties:** Children can produce their own estate agent leaflet or holiday brochure. They could try describing their own house or make a leaflet for the sale of the school. They could produce a promotional paragraph describing the locality, for example.

What's on the CD-ROM

On the CD-ROM you will find:
● Printable versions of all three photocopiable pages.
● Answers to 'Find the adjective in...'.
● Interactive version of 'Find the adjective in...'.

Identifying adjectives

Find the adjective in...

■ Look at these texts. Circle the words or phrases that are adjectives.

 This spacious house is situated on a charming, quiet road.
(Estate agent mailing)

 On top of a windy hill with nothing else to be friends with lived Something Else
(K. Cave 'Something Else')

 I took Dad's watch to pieces.
Mum said that I could.
I love these shiny wheels and things...
('The Watch Mender' by Michael Glover)

 'Is there anybody there?' said the Traveller,
Knocking on the moonlit door
('The Listeners' by Walter de la Mare)

 Moist tender coconut covered in thick milk chocolate.
('Bounty' advert)

 Torrential rains have caused a flood alert across the region.
(Local paper)

 He receives comfort like cold porridge.
(The Tempest)

 Don't miss this new series of scary stories.

 Thank you for the fantastic present. It was a brilliant surprise.

■ Can you write some new sentences using the same adjectives?

■SCHOLASTIC
www.scholastic.co.uk **PHOTOCOPIABLE** **Scholastic Literacy Skills**
Grammar and punctuation: Year 3 **63**

Name:

Identifying adjectives

Descriptive spaces

■ Where could you place an adjective in each of the sentences below? Could you place more than one adjective in each sentence?

■ Draw arrows in the spaces where you could put adjectives. Which ones would you add? The first one is done for you.

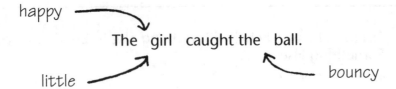

The bear hid behind a tree.

The boat crossed the river.

The wolf chased the duck.

The boy went on the bus to the shop.

My friend lives in a house in my street.

On the table at the party there was a cake.

The goblin lived in a den under the bridge.

The spaceship landed on the planet.

Identifying adjectives

Adjectives in poems

■ Find the adjectives in this poem. How important are they when you read the poem? Collect your thoughts in the table below.

Our Car

Our car's old
And very rusty.
It clangs and bangs
And rattles and
It's very dusty.
Dad's always got his head
Under the bonnet
And the roof's got lots
Of stains and dents upon it.
And in the mornings,
When it's cold,
It doesn't like starting,
And just coughs,
And coughs, and coughs…
But when I'm
In the back seat,
Strapped in, looking out,

I begin to think
I'm a racing driver,
And we're off…
And when it's dark,
I'm a spaceship captain,
Blasting through the stars.

I tell you,
I've really been far
In our old car.

Tony Bradman

Adjectives	My response

Text © 1989, Tony Bradman. Illustrations © 1999, Jane Cope.

Changing adjectives

Objective

Experiment with substituting adjectives in sentences.

Background knowledge

The range of adjectives that can be used is enormous and the subtleties of the range make them fascinating words to work with. The use of 'satisfactory' rather than 'good' to describe a meal or a piece of work is just one example of the way in which different adjectives, used in different ways, carry with them varying connotations. They are loaded words!

Activities

Through experimenting with the substitution of adjectives, children should develop their language use in two ways. Firstly, substitution reinforces the way in which adjectives are combined with other words and can be selected from a wide range. Secondly, substituting adjectives provides an interesting way of extending children's vocabulary. It is through substitution that children move beyond describing things merely as 'nice' to using other, more expressive words.

● **Photocopiable page 67 'Alternative adjectives'**
Through focusing upon well-known objects, children can try to list a variety of adjectives they could use to describe them.

● **Photocopiable page 68 'Match the adjective'**
This activity works backwards from various adjectives and asks children to consider which nouns could be described by them.

● **Photocopiable page 69 'Change the adjective'**
Once children have tried changing the adjectives in the text shown on the photocopiable sheet, they can try it with the various texts they encounter in shared and guided reading sessions.

Further ideas

● **Class thesaurus:** Using published thesauruses, children can look up commonly used adjectives such as 'good' and 'bad' and list alternatives that could be used. The examples could be bound into a class thesaurus.
● **Class rating:** Children can review their own writing and each other's to draw up a list of the most commonly used adjectives in their class. They could provide this auditing service to other teachers! Once they have drawn up this list they could use their class thesaurus to suggest alternatives.
● **Shared choice:** During shared writing activities, the class could experiment with the rule that they will not use an adjective until they have thought of two possibilities that could take the same place within a sentence.

What's on the CD-ROM

On the CD-ROM you will find:
● Printable versions of all three photocopiable pages.
● Interactive versions of 'Alternative adjectives' and 'Match the adjective'.

Changing adjectives

Alternative adjectives

■ Choose **eight** things you know well. Put one in the centre of each of the spiders below. At the end of each leg write an adjective to describe the thing. The first one is started for you.

old

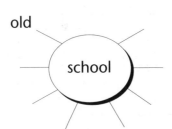

school

Suggestion box

school dinners	playtime
parties	clowns
books	computer
games	home
the shop	buses

my favourite television programme

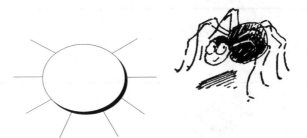

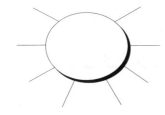

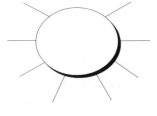

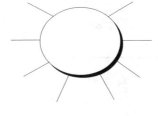

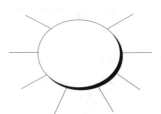

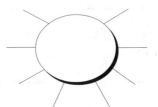

Illustrations © 1999, Jane Cope.

Name:

Changing adjectives

Match the adjective

■ Below is an adjective and something that the adjective describes. Can you think of **two** other things the adjective could describe? The first one has been done for you.

tall
tree   skyscraper   lamp-post

small
ant   _____   _____

green
traffic light   _____   _____

loud
jet plane   _____   _____

fast
comet   _____   _____

scary
spider   _____   _____

soft
tissue   _____   _____

cold
ice cube    _____   _____

bright
light bulb   _____   _____

tasty
chocolate   _____   _____

Illustrations © 1999, Jane Cope.

Changing adjectives

Change the adjective

■ Find the adjectives in this passage and circle them. Can you list them and suggest other adjectives that could take their place?

A dog barks and this cat with no name scrambles up a fence. This boy called Shane sees the little cat and yells, "Hey, you! Scaredycat!" The cat with no name hears the loud voice of the boy. And way up there on the top of the fence, this clever baby thing roll itself up. Such a tight little ball of fierce cat. It growls and then it spits right at the boy called Shane. Mad as anything!

From *Way Home* by Libby Hathorn

Adjective	Alternative adjective

Text © 1994, Libby Hawthorn. Illustrations © 1999, Jane Cope.

■ SCHOLASTIC
www.scholastic.co.uk   **PHOTOCOPIABLE**   **Scholastic Literacy Skills**
Grammar and punctuation: Year 3   **69**

Classifying adjectives

Objective

Collect and classify adjectives.

Background knowledge

There are several different kinds of adjectives. By far the largest class of adjectives modify nouns by describing qualities such as size, shape or colour, as in *big cat*, *round clock* and *blue book*.

There are also adjectives that modify nouns by indicating the quantity of a particular noun, for example *lots of cats*.

Other types of words such as demonstratives ('this', 'that'), possessives ('my', 'your') and interrogatives ('which', 'what') can be referred to as adjectives. They too modify nouns, as in *Look at these books* or *Look at my books*. Numerals are also classed as adjectives (as in *Bring me two books*).

Activities

The focus of these activities is the categories of adjective. This is a substantial task for children but provides a means of exploring the range of adjectives available to them.

● **Photocopiable page 71 'Types of adjective'**
This activity presents certain criteria that children can use to sort a set of adjectives. Once they have undertaken this activity they can try to adapt it, devising their own criteria for sorting adjectives. It could be as personal as 'adjectives we like' and 'adjectives we don't like'.

● **Photocopiable page 72 'Adjective machine'**
As a practice in using the adjective machine, children could run the adjectives from photocopiable page 71 'Types of adjective' through it.

● **Photocopiable page 73 'Devise the Thingy'**
Once they have devised and described their own 'Thingy' monsters, children can look at each other's and see if they can add to one another's list of adjectives used to describe the creatures.

Further ideas

● **Guessing:** Children can play a guessing game in which someone has to think of an item in the room and other children request types of adjective about the object, such as 'an adjective to describe its colour'. The questions are difficult to formulate and often result in some discussion. This game can also be played using objects on a tray with the class sitting in a circle around it.

● **Sets:** Write various adjectives on cards. Ask groups of children to devise their own criteria and sort the adjectives accordingly.

What's on the CD-ROM

On the CD-ROM you will find:
● Printable versions of all three photocopiable pages.
● Answers to 'Types of adjective'.
● Interactive version of 'Types of adjective'.

Classifying adjectives

Types of adjective

■ Read the phrases in these boxes. Each of them contains an adjective. Can you see what some of these adjectives have in common?

■ Cut out the boxes and sort them into those that contain:
  • adjectives that describe colour (such as 'red')
  • adjectives that describe mood and feeling (such as 'gloomy')
  • adjectives that describe size (such as 'tiny').

A big dog	A long road	A sad boy
A wide door	A scared man	A black coat
A purple shirt	A little boy	A miserable day
A blue sea	A wild party	A red shoe
An angry dog	A small flower	A green leaf
A happy girl	An orange orange	A brown dog
A tiny spider	A calm dog	A huge boat

Illustrations © 1999, Jane Cope.

Name:

Classifying adjectives

Adjective machine

- ■ Read through some texts and find some adjectives.
- ■ Can you find some adjectives that describe:
  - • how something looks (such as green)
  - • how something feels (such as rough)
  - • how something sounds (such as loud)
  - • how something tastes (such as chewy)?
- ■ Write some of the words you find in these spaces.

looks	feels	sounds	tastes

Illustrations © 1999, Jane Cope.

PHOTOCOPIABLE

Classifying adjectives

Devise the Thingy

This is a Thingy.

It is a big, warty, squeaky, spotted, smelly Thingy.

■ Can you invent **four** new Thingies? For each Thingy you need **at least three** adjectives.

■ Could you give your Thingies names? Could you use them in a story?

Illustrations © 1999, Jane Cope.

Adjectives in writing

Objective

Refine the use of adjectives in writing.

Writing focus

Through expanding and changing their choice of adjectives, children refine the quality of their sentence writing.

Skills to writing

● **Adjective rebounds**
Adjectives qualify nouns that could often stand on their own two feet, so as children develop their understanding of this class of word it is important that they consider the ways in which they could use them in their own writing. To do this they need 'adjective rebounds', where they experience the editing of their own work, revisiting sentences they have written and considering the adjectives they can use.

● **Persuasive adjectives**
Look for the use of adjectives in persuasive writing. Encourage children to bring in leaflets and adverts that are designed to sell a place or a product and find the various adjectives used to describe them. As they find these, ask them to consider how the adjective persuades us. What sort of image does it conjure up? Can they use this tactic in their own writing? Invites to class assembly or an open evening could be flowered up, for example.

● **Story description**
In story writing, encourage children to develop one or two paragraphs that give the best description they can fashion of the most important place or person in their text. If, for example, they are writing a story set in a fairy-tale palace, encourage them to spend time picturing and describing the palace. If it's a scary house, have them pick apart and describe various aspects of the setting. Ultimately, they want to get on and write a good story – so don't ask for too much. It's all about getting that one best description.

● **The big list**
Create a large list of adjectives on the wall, making project out of gathering and voting on the 30 words that will run from floor to ceiling. Involve the class in gathering and selecting the 30 then have them written up in bubbly and colourful lettering. Of all the vocabulary displays to have in a classroom, this is the vital one. Make sure there's a range of adjective types and keep referring to and altering the collection.

● **Synonym sorting**
Synonyms can be introduced through adjectives. Collect alternatives for basic adjectives like 'good' and 'bad', introducing children to the use of a thesaurus.

● **Poetry adjectives**
Poetry writing provides a good resource for locating and collecting adjectives. The poem 'The Listeners' is just one text that includes some great examples children can read and use to supply ideas for their own writing. When it comes to writing, simply gathering and shaping adjectives related to a subject can result in poetic sentences. These can be put together to create a free verse.

Activities

● **Photocopiable page 76 'Chocolate bar'**
This activity is best done after a week or two spent collecting real chocolate bar wrappers and looking at the slogans on them. A list could be kept of some of the best examples.

● **Photocopiable 77 'In your own words'**
This activity involves children looking at pieces of their own writing. As preparation, you may want to select pieces of writing that would best be applied to this activity.

Write on

● Adjective images

Children can write pictogram adjectives in big, graffiti-like letters and paint these, adding their own embellishments to match the word. For example, 'hot' can be a big red word that is sweating, whereas 'cold' can have a shape something like a set of icicles. Try words like 'deep', 'loud', 'sparkly' and 'happy'.

● Spooky

Following on from their reading of 'The Listeners', ask children to devise a spooky paragraph in which a character approaches a creepy house or mansion. As they do this they need to start with the nouns. Ask: *What would you enter through? What would you see? What would you hear?* Once they have planned these nouns, they need to reflect on the adjectives that would describe them. One step in between is to ask the children to devise the questions that will pick out adjectives. For example: If the door makes a noise, how does it sound? If there is a path, what are the brambles like at the side? The final step is to write a few sentences about the walk up the overgrown path with its scratchy branches to the creaking door.

● Thingy stories

Use the Thingies created on photocopiable page 73 'Devise the Thingy' in a story. Children can create a family, class or community of Thingies and devise stories about them. Encourage them to draw on the qualities they have described – so if one Thingy is lazy, let that be a part of their role in the story.

● Advert writing

Write and perform adverts as if the classroom was a television studio. Look at some current adverts for hair products, chocolates, drinks and so on, and ask the children to work in groups to devise their own suggestions for advert scripts. One important feature of this activity is to have a point on the wall that acts as the camera – children talk with confidence to the 'folks at home'.

What's on the CD-ROM

On the CD-ROM you will find:
- Printable versions of both photocopiable pages.

Name:

Adjectives in writing

Chocolate bar

■ Look at the chocolate bar below then try to devise two of your own. Notice that the slogan uses an adjective to describe the chocolate bar.

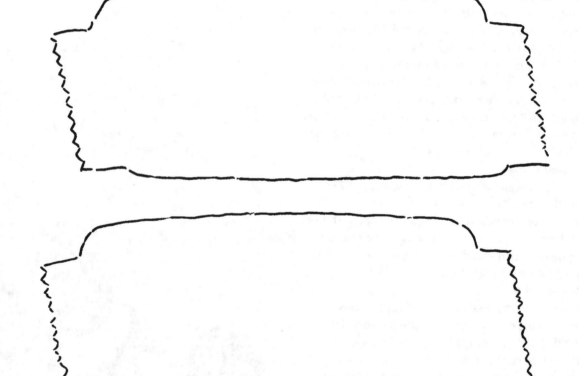

Illustrations © 1999, Jane Cope.

PHOTOCOPIABLE

Adjectives in writing

In your own words

■ Look at some pieces of writing you have done. Find some sentences that could have contained adjectives. Write the sentences in the first column.

■ Write each sentence again. This time, put in any adjectives that will make a better sentence.

Original	Redraft

Verbs

Introduction

This chapter will provide children with a thorough introduction to verbs. It includes activities that develop their understanding of the role verbs play in sentences. There is also a clear emphasis on trying things out with this class of words – particularly in the 'Verbs in writing' where children are encouraged to list and try out a variety of verbs. Children will be turned back on their own speech or environment to mime out examples they can then apply to their own writing.

Poster notes

Past, present and future (page 79)
This poster provides examples of the past and present tenses and the future form of a few common verbs. It can be displayed as a reminder of how these three tenses operate. Boxes or whole columns can be covered, leaving groups to suggest what the missing words could be. It illustrates important points about past and future tenses, which children soon notice when faced with the three columns.

Pin people (page 80)
This collection of pin people provides a variety of actions and the verbs that denote them. It is similar to the sort of chart children are asked to construct on photocopiable page 82 'Little boxes'.

In this chapter

Verbs

Past, present and future

In the past I	Now I	In the future I
walked	walk	will walk
ran	run	will run
crawled	crawl	will crawl
said	say	will say
sneezed	sneeze	will sneeze
thought	think	will think

Illustrations © 2008, Jane Cope.

Verbs

Pin people

PHOTOCOPIABLE

SCHOLASTIC
www.scholastic.co.uk

Collecting verbs

Learn the function of verbs in sentences, observing their key role in sentences.

Background knowledge

The verb is often considered to be the most important part of a sentence. It shows the action or state that is taking place.

● **Auxiliary verbs:** are sometimes called 'helping' verbs, they precede the main verb and make it conditional. For example, a sentence such as *I play ludo* is describing an action I actually do. If you add an auxiliary verb like 'can' to the sentence, *I can play ludo*, it says I can play it, not that I necessarily do.

● **Primary verbs:** are 'be', 'have' and 'do'. They can be main verbs – *I am running, I have a cold*, and *I did nothing*; or auxiliary verbs – *I was making a cake, I have told you once* and *I didn't see you*.

'Used', 'ought', 'need' and 'dare' can be used as auxiliaries or as verbs on their own (*I need a drink* and *I need to drink a drink*).

The other auxiliary verbs, are: 'can', 'could', 'may', 'might', 'must', 'will', 'shall', 'would' and 'should'. They always act as auxiliaries to other verbs.

Auxiliaries can often take the 'n't' contraction to make constructions like: 'haven't', 'wasn't' and 'can't'.

Activities

This section focuses on finding and identifying verbs in various contexts, whether it be rooting out ones that spring to mind when we are thinking about actions, or verbs we encounter in a range of texts.

● **Photocopiable page 82 'Little boxes'**
One of the most accessible ways for children to understand the function of verbs is to consider the words they use for various actions. This activity challenges them to generate as many different actions as they can. As the children complete this activity, they may present the same action with a different label (for example, two pictures of a runner, one labelled 'running' and the other labelled 'sprinting'). You may want to introduce them to the term *synonym* (two words with similar meanings such as 'hit' and 'whack' or 'cry' and 'weep'). It can be interesting to review the children's verbs after this activity to see which were the most common.

● **Photocopiable page 83 'Verb hunt'**
Children can encounter a range of verbs by looking at different types of text. This activity presents a range of texts and encourages the children to locate verbs. It is an activity that should naturally motivate the children to point out verbs in their immediate environment, such as those to be found in displays, notices, signs, and so on.

● **Photocopiable page 84 'Verbs in action'**
As an extension to the previous activity, children can use this photocopiable sheet to stick down and analyse material they extract from various texts in an effort to find a wide range of verbs. As they undertake this exercise, children can be shown the way in which every sentence they encounter requires a verb to make sense.

Further ideas

● **Synonyms:** Children can look back at photocopiable page 82 'Little boxes' and try to present a set of synonymous verbs for actions such as crying, falling and so on.

● **Synonyms in writing:** In their story writing, children can be encouraged to use synonymous verbs as a way of varying the language they use to describe actions.

● **Verbs in school:** Children can seek out verbs in the school environment, looking at notice-boards, signs and so on.

What's on the CD-ROM

On the CD-ROM you will find:
● Printable versions of all three photocopiable pages.
● Answers to 'Verb hunt'.
● An interactive version of 'Verb hunt'.

Name:

Collecting verbs

Little boxes

■   Think of different things people do. Draw as many different actions as you can in the boxes below and then write the name of the action in each box. Here are two examples.

running   skipping

■   Compare with a friend's little boxes. How many different verbs did you both use?

Illustrations © 1999, Jane Cope.

Collecting verbs

Verb hunt

■ Look for the verbs in these sentences. Remember that a verb can be a word or group of words. Draw a circle round any verbs you find.

■ Collect the verbs you have found. Look at someone else's collection. Did you find the same verbs?

■ How many of your verbs can you use in new sentences? Write some sentences with them.

Illustrations © 1999, Jane Cope.

Name:

Collecting verbs

Verbs in action

■ Look at different texts such as newspapers, leaflets, packages and so on. Cut out **eight** sentences and stick them in these spaces. Write out the verbs.

■ Use some other texts to find more verbs. Can you make a long list of the different verbs you find?

INSTRUCTIONS Open the green packet and remove the nuts and bolts. Before you	Open remove

Changing verbs

Objective

Learn the function of verbs in sentences, collecting and classifying examples and experimenting with changing them.

Background knowledge

One of the key processes in using language is selection. We select the right type of word to fit a place in a sentence. The code that guides our selection involves a number of features, including the need to make ourselves understood and the desire to choose a polite term. The way in which certain verbs will fit a particular context is a vital part of the reading process.

Activities

These activities focus on the way one verb can be selected from a family of verbs to describe a particular action. Attention is drawn to the connections that link certain verbs. This principle can be explored using a range of shared texts and collating examples of verbs that children use in their own writing.

● **Photocopiable page 86 'Verb links'**
One of the stylistic features of writing is the choice of a particular verb to cover a particular action or state. Through learning the close links within certain families of verbs, children reinforce their understanding of the type of word a verb is and build up their vocabulary. Encourage children to explore the range of standard and non-standard English expressions that they use to denote a particular action.

● **Photocopiable page 87 'Change the verb'**
This activity asks children to seek out an alternative verb to cover an action. It is this sort of thesaurus-like act of selection that can enrich writing. It also reinforces the reading skill of understanding the type of word that fits a particular context. Through exchanging the verbs in the sentences in this activity, children are developing their practical use of this skill.

● **Photocopiable page 88 'Our verbs'**
This activity revisits ground covered on photocopiable page 86 'Verb links'. It focuses children's attention on the verbs they use. The emphasis is on their vocabulary for the actions described. It could be an effective activity to do in pairs or groups, as this will often lead children to remind each other of verbs they have not considered. Point out that they can use verb phrases in which a few words denote the action (as in *blowing a gasket*).

Further ideas

● **Thesauruses:** Introduce children to the use of thesauruses in selecting an appropriate word for a particular action.
● **Definitive collections:** Can the class produce the definitive list of synonymous terms to cover a particular activity like 'snitching' (telling tales)? This could involve them looking beyond the classroom to ask parents, grandparents, teachers and so on for examples from their childhood.
● **Redrafting:** Children can apply the ideas in this section to their own writing, looking at verbs they commonly use. They can select a story they have written and consider whether they can improve the verbs they used.
● **Verb-pops:** A list of popular verbs can be maintained in the classroom. It can be a list of ten verbs encountered in stories that grabbed the interest of the children. They can nominate and vote on candidates for the list and alter it every so often. The raised profile of certain verbs will often lead children to use items on the list in preference to words to which they would have ordinarily resorted.

 What's on the CD-ROM

On the CD-ROM you will find:
● Printable versions of all three photocopiable pages.
● Answers to 'Change the verb'.
● Interactive version of 'Change the verb'.

Name:

Changing verbs

Verb links

■ At the centre of the spider diagrams below there is an action or a state. Write another word for that action at the end of each of the five legs.

■ Once you have completed these you could try drawing and completing your own verb links.

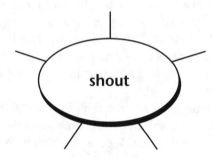

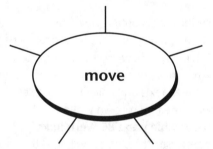

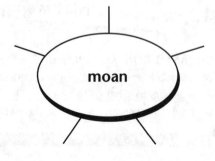

SCHOLASTIC
www.scholastic.co.uk

Changing verbs

Change the verb

■ Look at the sentences below. Each of them contains a verb. Cut out the sentences and swap the verb for a juicy verb.

■ Write your new sentence on a separate sheet of paper.

Juicy verbs		
slithered	bounced	shrieked
leaped	giggled	tumbled
dashed	halted	shattered
gobbled		pounced

Everyone	laughed	at the joke.
"Fire! Fire!"	the boy	said.
The snake	went	into the grass.
The window	broke	into many pieces.
The ball	went	down the stairs.
The tiger	came	out of the bushes.
The acrobats	moved	around the circus ring.
We	ran	for safety.
The train	stopped	before the broken bridge.
The frog	went	into the water.
The greedy goblin	ate	all the food.

Name:

Changing verbs

Our verbs

When I am playing with my friend and I want us to run I say *"Leggit"*.

When I'm moaning my Mum tells me to stop *mithering*.

We use different words for the same activity. Sometimes these verbs are special to our family or the area in which we live.

■ Look at the boxes below. Write in each box a list of words you could use for the action.

running away	moaning	being sick
scarper	whingeing	spewing

getting angry	being silly	getting told off
blowing a gasket	larking about	getting done

PHOTOCOPIABLE

SCHOLASTIC
www.scholastic.co.uk

Tenses

Understand the appropriate and consistent use of verb tenses.

Background knowledge

The tense is the grammatical category, expressed in forms of the verb, which locates an action in time. In English there are two simple tenses:
- **Present tense:** the action is occurring now (*I walk*)
- **Past tense:** the action occurred previously. The common ending for past-tense verbs is 'ed' (*I walked*).

For these two tenses the verb stem itself can alter. There is a third, more complex tense, this is:
- **Future tense:** is made in a compound form (another word is added to set a verb in the future). In the above example, the simple present has the word 'will' added, creating the compound form *will walk*.

Activities

The first two activities in this section look at the way the verb alters to indicate a change in tense. The third activity considers how an action is presented as happening in the future. It is worth clarifying the difference between the simple tenses of past and present and the compound nature of the future tense.
- **Photocopiable page 90 'Verb pairs'**
This activity involves children matching verbs of differing tenses. The activity could be extended to involve them sticking the two columns they make onto a large sheet of paper so that they can be compared side by side.
- **Photocopiable page 91 'Tense changer'**
In each of these examples, children can simply change the verb to alter the tense. Some may suggest changes such as *I was hiding* for the past tense of *I hide* (this is, in fact, the imperfect or past continuous tense). Point out that the activity can work without adding any new words, just changing the ones we have. Bear in mind that each of the examples involves the first-person singular doing the action.

- **Photocopiable page 92 'Past to future'**
This activity introduces the compound form of the future tense. If appropriate, you could introduce the term *compound* with the class. Whether you introduce the term or not, it is important to point out the different type of change being made here: to make the future we add another word before the verb.

Further ideas

- **Stories:** Look at different types of story telling and the uses of tense in narrative. The predominant one is the past tense. However, there are examples of stories told in the present tense. Some oral storytellers use it to create the scene before your eyes. It is also common in jokes (*This rabbit walks into a shop and buys some carrots…*).
- **Altering tenses:** Use sentences from texts and retell them in the present or future tenses, looking at the alteration that is made.
- **Diary sentences:** Ask children to offer examples of things that they do throughout the school day (such as *We go to assembly*, *We paint a picture*) and then rephrase these in the past tense, as if they were written in a diary.
- **Big change/Little change:** Introduce children to the nature of the alteration made to verbs when they switch from present to past tense. Verbs like 'I walk' just have the '-ed' morpheme added to make 'walked'. However, some verbs (like 'I go') change completely. On photocopiable page 91 'Tense changer' there is one verb that doesn't change its appearance at all. Ask the children to look for verbs that alter completely and those that just have additions to the end of the verb.

What's on the CD-ROM

On the CD-ROM you will find:
- Printable versions of all three photocopiable pages.
- Answers to all three photocopiable pages.
- Interactive versions of 'Verb pairs' and 'Tense changer'.

Name:

Tenses

Verb pairs

■ Cut out the verbs below. Can you find a present tense and past tense of the same verb? Place them alongside each other.

■ When you have finished make up some pairs of your own.

watched	shout	stop	bit	see
wrote	find	ran	play	won
type	walked	helped	swam	stopped
run	made	win	ate	walk
shouted	help	write	saw	bite
found	eat	typed	draw	played
swim	drew	make	watch	

Illustrations © 1999, Jane Cope.

Tenses

Tense changer

■ Complete this grid. You need to change the past-tense verbs into present tense and the present-tense verbs into past tense.

■ Can you think of some other verbs and their different tenses? Make a list on the back of this sheet.

Past	Present
I found	
I lived	
	I am
	I do
	I cut
I said	
	I hide
I chased	
	I make
	I hear
I ate	
	I change
I chose	
	I sing
I jumped	
	I write
I stopped	
I fell	
I moved	
	I work
I opened	
	I spill
I thought	
I brought	
	I bite
I called	

Illustrations © 1999, Jane Cope.

Name:

Past to futre

Tenses

■ These sentences are written in the past tense. Rewrite them in the present and future tenses.

Yesterday Sam went to school.

Today _____

Tomorrow _____

Yesterday he walked to school.

Today _____

Tomorrow _____

Yesterday I ate my lunch.

Today _____

Tomorrow _____

Yesterday I had a banana.

Today _____

Tomorrow _____

■ Now try some of your own past to future sentences.

Illustrations © 1999, Jane Cope.

Investigating verbs

Objective

Learn to consider the functions of verbs in sentences.

Background knowledge

These activities revise previous knowledge of verbs, including the way in which verbs are essential components of sentences, the links between various verbs, and the process of selecting the most appropriate verb in the right context.

One of the outcomes of working on verbs can be a change in the verbs selected in writing. Look at the writing the children engage in throughout the day and across the curriculum.

Activities

The idea underpinning this section is that every sentence needs a verb and the selection of that verb makes a difference to the whole sentence. By looking at verbless sentences, the necessity of the verb to convey the overall meaning is re-emphasised. The children look at links between verbs and at the use of specific verbs in a classic text.

● **Photocopiable page 94 'Can't without one'**
Ask the children to look at these sentences and find where they think a verb could be inserted and decide what verb it could be. They can then compare their results. There will probably be a consistent response to where the verbs should be placed but there may be some variety in the verbs that are selected. This could lead to discussion about the type of verb we usually employ to describe an action. For example, *The girl…a goal* could be *The girl scored a goal* but probably not *The girl made a goal*.

● **Photocopiable page 95 'Verb to verb'**
By linking the verbs, children revisit the familiar nature of verbs and begin to explore the links between them.

● **Photocopiable page 96 'Looking at a story'**
Share in the reading of this text from Oscar Wilde's *The Selfish Giant*. Children can:
● find the verbs in the passage
● look at the verbs that are used and suggest alternatives that could have been used
● consider the effects of the particular verb used.
● The passage has been selected because of the careful use of verbs in describing the various actions.

Further ideas

● **Redrafting:** Children can look at samples of writing they have done in order to focus on the following redrafting activity. Ask the children to find a verb they have used. Can they think of two other verbs that could have been placed in that context? Which verb will they select as the best for that context? Can they explain why you chose that verb?

● **Collecting verbs:** Children can maintain a collection of verbs that fit within the families explored on photocopiable page 95 'Verb to verb'. Charts or pages in a loose leaf folder can be maintained, to which new examples of verbs under each heading can be added, as children encounter new examples in various texts.

What's on the CD-ROM

On the CD-ROM you will find:
● Printable versions of all three photocopiable pages.
● Answers to 'Can't without one!' and 'Verb to verb'.
● Interactive version of 'Verb to verb'.

Name:

Investigating verbs

Can't without one!

■ Each of these sentences has a verb missing. Can you guess what it is and mark where it should go?

The chicken away from the fox.

I my lost keys.

The girl a goal.

The boy into the swimming pool.

The sun shining.

Can you me a story?

A bird up into a tree.

The red monster the green monster.

We pictures of our faces.

The cow the grass.

Yesterday it Tuesday.

The man the car.

■ Can you write your own verbless sentences for your friends to try and solve?

_____

_____

_____

Investigating verbs

Verb to verb

■ The verbs below are all connected in families. There are different words linked to: speaking, seeing, holding and falling.

■ Can you shade each verb family in a different colour?

whispered   glimpsed   held   tumble   saw   clasped

clapped eyes on   clutched   stumbled   stated

shouted   spotted   gripped   toppled   noticed   grabbed

observed   shrieked   clung onto   tripped

plunged   grasped   expressed   collapsed   discussed

plummeted   spied   tugged   talked   looked   told

■ Collect the different families together and write the verbs in the boxes.

Speaking	Seeing	Holding	Falling

Investigating verbs

Looking at a story

■ Read this story. Look at the verbs that are used and consider their affect.

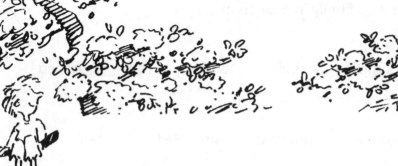

The Selfish Giant

"I believe the Spring has come at last," said the Giant; and he jumped out of bed and looked out.

What did he see?

He saw a most wonderful sight. Through a little hole in the wall the children had crept in, and they were sitting in the branches of the trees. In every tree that he could see there was a little child. And the trees were so glad to have the children back again that they had covered themselves with blossoms, and were waving their arms gently above the children's heads. The birds were flying about twittering with delight, and the flowers were looking up through the green grass and laughing. It was a lovely scene, only in one corner it was still winter.

From *The Selfish Giant* by Oscar Wilde

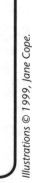

Illustrations © 1999, Jane Cope.

PHOTOCOPIABLE

■SCHOLASTIC
www.scholastic.co.uk

Verbs in writing

Objective

Expand use of verbs in writing.

Writing focus

Moving from the most obvious choices for verbs in their writing, children try out a variety of verbs that add interest.

Skills to writing

● **Verbs in stories**
Verbs are a great means of getting children thinking about stories – translating their enjoyment of their reading into more imaginative writing. Take a look at some of the illustrations in the picture books that are firm favourites within the school and cover the text. Ask the children to come up with some verbs that label the actions in the pictures. This can provide an interesting way of summarising the key events of a story. Ask questions such as *What five verbs would retell the story of Cinderella?*

● **Verb summaries**
Having used verbs to summarise stories, children can also use them for planning their own narrative writing. Before they write a story, ask them to list the five verbs that will summarise the stages of their story. This can lead to a chance to look up and consider some synonyms and more interesting vocabulary.

● **Try a verb on**
Try verbs on. Trying a new word is never as simple as substituting one word found in a thesaurus for another. As children encounter new words for an action like 'speak', they need to know the difference between a synonym like 'tell' and one like 'accost'. As they encounter new verbs, take time to try them on, seeking out opportunities for the new word over the course of a school day – possibly even tallying up the amount of use it receives.

● **Collections**
Collect a selection of verbs that can be used in writing. Encourage the children to look out for interesting sounding verbs in sentences they hear or read. These can be collected and stored for use in writing. Particular focus could be placed on words for movement ('ran', 'dashed', 'sauntered') and speech ('yelled', 'whispered', 'murmured') as these will prove to be a good resource in narrative writing. Other good collections can include words for seeking, finding, understanding and seeing.

● **Imperative instructing**
Use of the imperative verb is an important feature of instructional writing. Again, verbs can provide a good planning tool, with children itemising these as a way of staging out the process they will be writing. Watch out for children writing activities they know well or have done as instructional texts – it is very common for them to lapse into past tense narrative mode.

Activities

● **Photocopiable page 99 'Looking at verbs in stories'**
By looking at the way in which writers use verbs to create an effect, children should both appreciate the texts they read and build up the stock of words they can use in their own writing.

● **Photocopiable page 100 'Advertising Zesto'**
One of the areas of language use in which words are carefully selected is advertising. In this activity, children need to take on an editorial role and imagine each of the texts is an idea presented to them from which they must make the best advertisement. It is crucial that they remember their audience. They need to think of the sort of people who drink fizzy drinks and decide upon the words that would sell Zesto to them. Once they have made their selections it can be useful to gather a class together and see which words they selected. Are the advertisements they designed similar? Are there certain points on which they all differ?

Write on

- **Megalists**

Make large lists of all the various terms for the actions on photocopiable page 88 'Our verbs'. Children can work in groups and see how long they can make their lists. They may want to ask other people to contribute terms.

- **Try the movement**

As children learn new words for moving and speaking they can try them out in drama activities. They can try 'creeping' or 'sauntering', as well as 'yelling' and 'sneering'.

- **Ad-verb-tising**

Having looked at the advert for Zesto, children can devise their own wonder products and adverts – possibly linking to the previous work on adjectives. One variation is to advertise magical and weird products, where the resultant contrasting verbs will be dynamic. They can think of the sort of before and after verbs they would put into an advert, such as one for invisibility cream or flying potion. Adverts can then be written up and presented to the class, like the adverts on the photocopiable sheet.

- **Unusual instructions**

Instructional texts needn't be about mundane jobs that children will have done. Ask them to write an instructional booklet containing lessons for young wizards, advice on 'How to use a broomstick' or a guide for new secret agents, 'How to use your gadgets'.

- **School of the future**

Flex those future tenses by writing up imaginative report texts on what it will be like in the school of the future. How will children travel there? What will lessons look like? What sort of teachers will they have? What will happen at playtime? As children write up their future-tense texts, they could also consider what might be the same. What won't change over the coming 100 years?

What's on the CD-ROM

On the CD-ROM you will find:
- Printable versions of both photocopiable pages.
- An interactive version of 'Advertising Zesto'.

Verbs in writing

Looking at verbs in stories

■ Look through some story books to find different verbs. Try to find verbs that describe:
- ways of speaking ('whispered', 'shrieked')
- ways of moving ('ran', 'dived')
- ways of seeing ('glimpsed', 'spied')
- ways of having ('held', 'grabbed').

■ Sort the verbs you find into the spaces below.

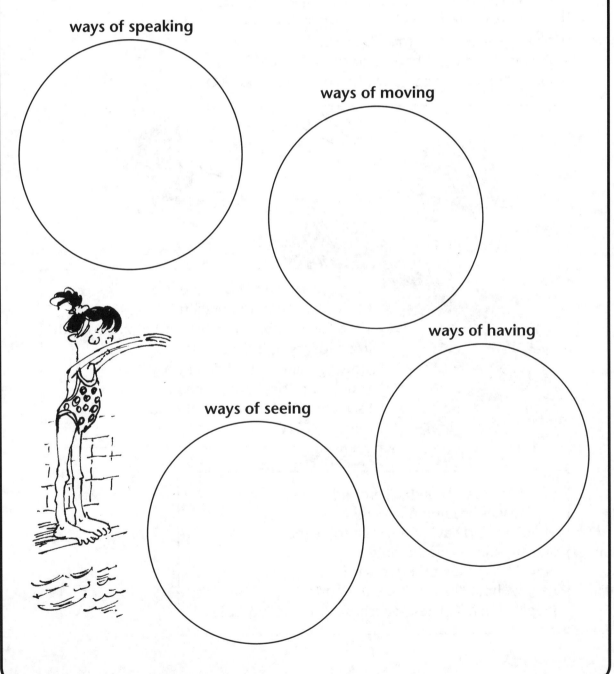

ways of speaking

ways of moving

ways of having

ways of seeing

Illustrations © 1999, Jane Cope.

Name:

Verbs in writing

Advertising Zesto

■ Look at these three versions of the same advertisement. Circle the words that change. Underline which word is best. Can you think of any better words to use?

■ Create your own version.

I used to slouch and plod around.
My life was going nowhere.
Then I started drinking new 'Zesto' filled with fizz and bursting from the bottle.
Now I leap about. I smile. I dance.
People ask "Hey! What's happened?"
I say "I'm full of zest – because I'm drinking ZESTO!"

I used to walk and crawl around.
My life was turning nowhere.
Then I started buying new 'Zesto' packed with fizz and fizzing from the bottle.
Now I go about. I smirk. I bop.
People say "Hey! What's changed?"
I scream "I'm full of zest – because I'm buying ZESTO!"

I used to stumble and fall around.
My life was heading nowhere.
Then I started having new 'Zesto' made with fizz and shooting from the bottle.
Now I bound about. I grin. I move.
People shout "Hey! What's altered?"
I reply "I'm full of zest – because I'm guzzling ZESTO!"

Illustrations © 1999, Jane Cope.

PHOTOCOPIABLE

■ SCHOLASTIC
www.scholastic.co.uk

Chapter 5

Making sentences

Introduction

This chapter takes a basic look at sentences, concentrating on their punctuation. It builds upon the elementary punctuation marks – demarcating sentences with capital letters and an ending mark such as question marks, exclamation marks or full stops. It also develops the use of inverted commas and commas in lists. 'Punctuation in writing' then uses the sentence as a tool for composition and revision.

In this chapter

Basic punctuation page 104	Consolidate understanding of sentence punctuation.
Commas and inverted commas page 108	Apply punctuation in writing. Learn to use commas in lists and inverted commas.
Speech marks page 112	Use speech marks and other dialogue punctuation.
Sentences working together page 116	Use commas to mark grammatical boundaries in sentences.
Punctuation in writing page 120	Apply punctuation in writing.

Poster notes

Punctuation (page 102)
The list of punctuation marks encountered in the chapter is complemented by a list of sentences. In the various sentences, children will find examples of the punctuation marks referred to in the list.

Punctuation checklist (page 103)
This poster can act as a checklist for children to apply to their writing. It narrows down to a small set of questions with a view towards simplifying the revision task children face as they re-read their texts.
It should be modelled using shared and guided writing and one added use is to see if children start to remember the five questions without needing to refer to the poster.

Making sentences

Punctuation

- **the capital letter**
The children were messing about.

- **the full stop**
We made spinners at school.

- **the question mark**
How do you make a spinner?

- **commas in lists**
To make a spinner you will need paper,
sticky tape, string and tissue paper.

- **speech marks**
Sam said "Don't jump on the settee."

- **the exclamation mark**
Don't jump on the settee!

Illustrations © 2008, Jane Cope.

PHOTOCOPIABLE

SCHOLASTIC
www.scholastic.co.uk

Making sentences

Punctuation checklist

Illustrations © 2008, Jane Cope.

Basic punctuation

Objective

Consolidate understanding of sentence punctuation.

Background knowledge

The items of punctuation covered in these activities are the capital letter, the full stop, the question mark and commas in lists. (The capital letter is, strictly speaking, not a punctuation mark, but is taught at the same time as the full stop.) Children may also demonstrate awareness of speech marks and exclamation marks.

Punctuation emerges through children's writing as it develops. Children will often write sentences that should include certain items of punctuation but omit the actual marks. The emphasis here is on activities that help to draw out the individual child's awareness of punctuation.

Activities

These activities present an opportunity for children to revise and consolidate their awareness of punctuation.

● **Photocopiable page 105 'Check these out'**
The sentences provided in this activity will accommodate the use of capital letters, full stops, question marks, commas, inverted commas and an exclamation mark.

● **Photocopiable page 106 'The hot-seat'**
As the children respond to the questions, remind them that they are to answer in sentences. A sentence can be defined as 'a unit of written language which makes sense on its own'. The children should use this definition to check that their answers are written as sentences. For example, if a child responds to the first question with 'Rafi', an individual word, it holds no real meaning on its own as it is out of context. A response as a sentence such as *My name is Rafi,* makes sense in its own right and so fits the definition.

● **Photocopiable page 107 'Recycle the words'**
This activity gives children the opportunity to devise sentences of their own. The words in the bins can be used to produce examples of punctuated sentences. The children should consider the various types of demarcation they can use. The results can be compared to look at how children used their words.

Further ideas

● **Punctuation finding:** Children can look through texts to find the different types of punctuation used. Can they figure out from these contexts the functions of various punctuation marks (such as parentheses)?
● **Question setting:** Children can follow on from photocopiable page 106 'The hot-seat' by setting their own questions for others in the class to answer. A questions-board could be established on which children can pin a question they would like to ask a member of the class. A variation of this activity is to ask children to look at the board and answer a chosen number of questions that it poses.
● **Recycles:** Photocopiable page 107 'Recycle the words' can be adapted to use a new set of words. This can work well if vocabulary from a particular topic is included (such as science: 'gravity', 'force'). Children can then use their developing subject knowledge to devise a set of questions.

What's on the CD-ROM

On the CD-ROM you will find:
● Printable versions of all three photocopiable pages.
● Answers to 'Check these out'.
● Interactive versions of 'Check these out' and 'Recycle the words'.

Basic punctuation

Check these out

■ Rewrite these sentences with the correct punctuation.

i can see my friend

_____

can we go to the park

_____

is it raining

_____

we are going to the park

_____

my favourite colours are red purple pink and orange

_____

stacey said race you to the corner

_____

can you see my friend

_____

i said boo to my mum

_____

stop look listen before you cross the road

_____

Basic punctuation

Name:

The hot-seat

■ Answer the following questions about yourself in full sentences.

What is your name?

_____

Where do you live?

_____

What are your favourite colours?

_____

What is your favourite place?

_____

Where did you go last weekend?

_____

What is the last programme you saw on television?

_____

What do you like doing at school?

_____

Where is your favourite place?

_____

What do you like about your favourite place?

_____

■ Can you write some questions to ask your friends?

_____

_____

PHOTOCOPIABLE ■SCHOLASTIC
www.scholastic.co.uk

Basic punctuation

Recycle the words

■ These words have been thrown away. Can you use the words in each bin to make a new sentence? Say each sentence aloud then write down some of them.

Commas and inverted commas

Objective

Learn to use commas in lists and inverted commas.

Background knowledge

Within sentences, commas and speech marks form two of the most basic units of punctuation. Speech marks, or inverted commas, are used to demarcate speech in written text. They appear in pairs around the actual words spoken.

Within speech marks the first word spoken is demarcated by a capital letter. In a sentence like: *Sam said "Don't jump on the settee"* the first spoken word is a capital. However, if the speech is broken, as in: *"Don't," said Sam, "jump on the settee"* the second part of the speech does not begin with a capital.

Among other uses, commas are used to separate items in lists, as in: *To make a spinner you will need paper, sticky tape, string and tissue paper.* In this context, they are not usually used after the penultimate item in a list.

Activities

Once children are clear about the demarcation of sentences they can start looking at items to demarcate *within* sentences. Speech marks and commas in lists form two clear examples they can identify.

● **Photocopiable page 109 'Speech shading'**
In this activity, the children identify speech in texts. The texts for this activity are taken from: the scene in which the Duck discovers he is free from the tyranny of the farmer in *Farmer Duck* by Martin Waddell (Walker Books); the meeting of Eddie and the Bear, each carrying the other's teddy in *Where's My Teddy?* by Jez Alborough (Walker Books); the conversation amongst the owls left alone from *Owl Babies* by Martin Waddell (Walker Books). All of these are available as Big Books.

● **Photocopiable page 110 'Lists with commas'**
By creating normal and sentence lists in this activity children will put the idea of commas in lists into practice. Some children may want to try making sentences with lists at the start, as in: *Red, green and blue are my favourite colours.*

● **Photocopiable page 111 'You will need'**
Taking some straightforward examples, this activity asks children to look at the format of sentence lists and try making their own.

Further ideas

● **Story speech:** Children can try using the speech from picture books like *Farmer Duck* to create a short drama piece acting out the story. Point out that they can find their lines for their drama by looking for the spoken words demarcated in the text.

● **Procedural texts:** Looking at various sorts of procedural texts, children can look to see how the 'You will need' bit is organised. They could find some that are organised as lists and remodel them as sentences.

What's on the CD-ROM

On the CD-ROM you will find:
● Printable versions of all three photocopiable pages.
● Answers to 'Speech shading'.
● An interactive version of 'Lists with commas'.

Commas and inverted commas

Speech shading

■ Look at these passages from stories.
Some of these words were said by characters in the story.
For example, in

> The duck answered "Quack!".

the duck said the word, Quack.

■ Using a colouring pencil, gently shade over the words that were actually spoken.

The duck awoke and waddled wearily into the yard
expecting to hear, How goes the work?
But nobody spoke!
Then the cow and the sheep and the hens came back.
Quack? asked the duck.
Moo! said the cow.
Baa! said the sheep.
Cluck! said the hens.
Which told the duck the whole story.

     from *Farmer Duck* by Martin Waddell

MY TED! gasped the bear.
A BEAR! screamed Eddy.
A BOY! yelled the bear.
MY TEDDY! cried Eddy.

     from *Where's My Teddy?* by Jez Alborough

One night they woke up and their owl mother was GONE.
Where's Mummy? asked Sarah.
Oh my goodness! said Percy.
I want my Mummy! said Bill.
The baby owls thought
(all owls think a lot) –
I think she's gone hunting, said Sarah.
To get us our food! said Percy.
I want my Mummy! said Bill.

     from *Owl Babies* by Martin Waddell

Owl Babies text © 1991, Martin Waddell; Where's my teddy? Text © 1992, Jez Alborough; Farmer Duck text © 1991, Martin Waddell. Illustrations © 1999, Jane Cope.

Name:

Commas and inverted commas

List with commas

Look at this list.

To make a cake you need:
Flour
Butter
Sugar
Eggs

It can be written as a sentence.

To make a cake you need flour, butter, sugar and eggs.

Look at the commas. They can separate items in a list. You don't need a comma to separate the last two items in the list. The word 'and' is doing this.

■ Try making your own lists of these groups. Write **four** items in each list.

teachers	**tasty foods**	**farmyard animals**	**points on the compass**
things you have in your classroom		**things you can do at playtime**	

■ Turn your lists into sentences.

Four of our teachers are _____

Four tasty foods are _____

Four farmyard animals are _____

Four points of the compass are _____

In our classroom we have _____

At playtime we can _____

■ Try making up some sentence lists about other things. Here are some ideas to get you started.

places to go	**people in your family**	**things you can do**
names you like	**good television programmes**	
things you can make	**colours**	**favourite sweets**

PHOTOCOPIABLE

Illustrations © 1999, Jane Cope.

■**SCHOLASTIC**
www.scholastic.co.uk

Commas and inverted commas

You will need

■ Look at these lists of things you will need for various activities.

> To make a cake you will need flour, eggs, sugar and vanilla essence.

> To make a kite you will need plain paper, tissue paper, string and sticky tape.

> To play 'Pin the tail on the donkey' you will need a blindfold, a pin, a large sheet of paper and a thick felt-tipped pen.

■ Try devising your own.

To _____

you will need _____

To _____

you will need _____

To _____

you will need _____

> Don't forget to separate things with a comma.

Illustrations © 1999, Jane Cope.

Speech marks

Objective

Use speech marks and other dialogue punctuation.

Background knowledge

Speech marks are used to demarcate the words that were actually spoken in a sentence. In a sentence like *Mum said, "Tidy up"* the speech marks enclose the words Mum actually said.

Lines of speech can be separated from the words denoting who is speaking in three ways: The speech can come after the other words: *Mum said, "Can you lot go and tidy your room?"* or before them: *"Can you lot go and tidy your room?" Mum said.* Or the speech can be separated by other words: *"Can you lot go," Mum said, "and tidy your room."*

In each of these, the speech marks enclose the actual words said. Commas are also used to mark the gap between a set of words that are spoken and other words.

Activities

The emphasis in these activities is upon the use of speech marks, though the use of commas in such sentences can also be pointed out. The main idea to get across is the way in which speech marks enclose words that were actually said. This idea can be communicated by envisaging the speech marks as being like a bubble that has been rubbed out leaving the marks behind.

● **Photocopiable page 113 'Marking out speech'**
As they read the poem 'Overheard on a Saltmarsh', children can try figuring out which of the two speakers is saying the individual lines. This activity can act as a prelude to other reading activities. The piece can be read by two groups taking the parts of the two characters, or the teacher can read one part and the children respond with the other.

● **Photocopiable page 114 'Speech marks'**
By remodelling the scripted passage as dialogue, children get experience of trying a range of words to describe the act of speaking.

● **Photocopiable page 115 'Speech marks 2'**
As they try to demarcate the words in the sentences, children will need to figure out which words were actually spoken.

Further ideas

● **Carpet talk:** During class discussions, explain to the class that, over the coming week, they are occasionally going to stop a speaker after they have said something and ask the class to figure out how that act of speaking would be recorded in an account of the event written later on. For the next week, every so often, after a child has said something like *Can I take the register downstairs?*, stop the class and ask them to model the event as a sentence on the board (for example, *Fozia asked, "Can I take the register downstairs?"*).

● **Dialogue:** Children can find passages in novels in which a group of characters are speaking and try acting out the passage, each taking a role and saying aloud the words ascribed to that character.

● **Ways of saying:** Children can think of as many different ways of saying something as they can. Examples could include 'shrieking', 'sneering' and so on. They can try speaking in this way and deciding which words they would use to denote that manner of speaking.

What's on the CD-ROM

On the CD-ROM you will find:
● Printable versions of all three photocopiable pages.
● Answers to 'Marking out speech' and 'Speech marks 2'.
● An interactive version of 'Speech marks 2'.

Speech marks

Marking out speech

■ There are two speakers in this poem – a nymph and a goblin.
Read the poem carefully.
■ Can you work out which lines the goblin is saying? Can you work out which lines the nymph is saying?
■ Shade over the nymph's lines in one colour and the goblin's lines in another.

Overheard on a Saltmarsh

Nymph, nymph, what are your beads?
Green glass, goblin. Why do you stare at them?
Give them me.
                    No.
Give them me. Give them me.
                    No.
Then I will howl all night in the reeds,
Lie in the mud and howl for them.

Goblin, why do you love them so?

They are better than stars or water,
Better than voices of winds that sing,
Better than any man's fair daughter,
Your green glass beads on a silver ring.

Hush, I stole them out of the moon.

Give my your beads, I desire them.
                    No.
I will howl in a deep lagoon
For your green glass beads, I love them so.
Give them me. Give them me.
                    No.

Harold Monro

Text © 1922, Harold Munro. Illustrations © 1999, Jane Cope.

■ SCHOLASTIC
www.scholastic.co.uk   **PHOTOCOPIABLE**   **Scholastic Literacy Skills**
Grammar and punctuation: Year 3   **113**

Name:

Speech marks

Speech marks

■ Look at the conversation below.

Lou's voice   **Sam's voice**

Wake up. It's time for school.

You have to go to school.

You have to go!

You still have to get up for school.

For a very good reason.

You're the headteacher.

I don't want to go to school.

But all the children hate me.

But all the teachers hate me.

Why do I have to get up for school?

What is it?

■ Turn over this sheet and rewrite the conversation as a passage with speech. A start has been made for you here.

"Wake up. It's time for school," said Lou.

"I don't want to go to school," grumbled Sam.

Speech words to help you		
said	called	grumbled
	shouted	mumbled
	yelled	moaned

PHOTOCOPIABLE

Speech marks

Speech marks 2

■ These lines have lost their speech marks. Can you rewrite them putting the speech marks in? Change letters that should be capitals and add any other missing punctuation.

■ The final example is much more difficult. Write it out correctly on the back of this sheet.

quick said sam hide the map

help me clean up this mess josh said

hey you the teacher shouted where are you going

can I tidy the art corner the boy asked the teacher

my sock is smellier than yours joe said to sam no it isn't sam replied

boo shouted the girl eek screamed her mum oh you gave me a fright

go away said the scarecrow you can't make us the birds replied can't i he shouted

give us a sweet leah snapped no replied josh ask politely ok leah said please give us a sweet that's better said josh

Sentences working together

● Photocopiable page 118 'What commas separate'
This activity can be undertaken using the *Granny* passage on the previous photocopiable sheet. Alternatively, other sentences can be looked at with a view towards investigating the use of the comma.

● Photocopiable page 119 'Commas slot bits in'
The main idea in this activity is the way commas mark inserted clauses. It is as if the insert has pushed the sentence apart, leaving the commas as fingerprints. Children can return clauses to their places. They can also look at how the sentence can make sense without the inserted clause. They could see whether this rule applies to other sentences they find with inserted clauses.

Objective

Use commas to mark grammatical boundaries in sentences.

Background knowledge

Among other uses, commas can be used to:
● **Separate items in a list:** *I like coffee, cakes, chocolate and oranges.* (See Commas and inverted commas on page 108.)
● **Separate clauses in sentences:** *I left the house, not realising I had no shoes on.* (See below.)
● **Mark out clauses inserted in sentences:** *I left the house, planning to be five minutes, and walked to the bus stop.* (See below.)

Clauses are distinct parts of sentences that say something complete in themselves. In some ways, they are like individual sentences. In the above example, the leaving of the house is a separate fact to the lack of realisation I was shoeless. Similarly, the inserted part of the third example states, separately to the rest, that I planned to be five minutes. Commas can separate off these clauses.

Further ideas

● **Sentence shading:** Looking at sentences in which clauses are separated by commas, children can try shading over the separate clauses to highlight the different meanings each one carries.
● **Reviewing writing:** Following these activities, children can re-read pieces of writing from the first part of this year and look at sentences they would organise differently. Specifically, they can look for sentences that could have had more complexity to them and in which they could have placed other clauses.

Activities

By Year 3, children are ready to demarcate more within sentences. There comes a stage in their writing at which the stream of words they produce needs putting into separate sentences. Once this target is achieved there is then a need to extend the sentences from within, otherwise children end up with staccato pieces of writing made up of short sentences. Through beginning to use commas, children begin to demarcate within sentences.

● Photocopiable page 117 'Commas and clauses'
Once they have read this passage from Anthony Horowitz's *Granny* and investigated the use of commas, children can apply the same idea to other texts. The activity works well with extracts from novels.

What's on the CD-ROM

On the CD-ROM you will find:
● Printable versions of all three photocopiable pages.
● Answers to 'Commas slot bits in'.
● An interactive version of 'Commas slot bits in'.

Commas and clauses

■ Commas can separate different parts of a sentence.

■ In each of these sentences from a story, two things are being said in one sentence. These are two clauses.

■ Read each sentence and look at the way the comma separates the two clauses.

Briefly, he scanned the food that lay before him.

There it was, the same as always.

First, there were egg mayonnaise sandwiches, but the eggs had been left out so long that the yellows had taken on a greenish tint.

Granny's home made cakes were dry and heavy, guaranteed to glue the top of your mouth to the bottom of your mouth with little taste in between.

She put the serviettes down and picked up a green porcelain bowl, filled to the brim with thick cream cheese.

Finally she slid the whole thing towards him and as she did so Joe saw the trembling half-smile on her lips, the rattlesnake eyes that pinned him to his seat.

He looked at the cream cheese, slooping about in the bowl with the herring lying there like a dead slug.

From *Granny* by Anthony Horowitz

Text © 1994, Anthony Horowitz.

■SCHOLASTIC
www.scholastic.co.uk   **PHOTOCOPIABLE**   **Scholastic Literacy Skills**
                                                    Grammar and punctuation: Year 3   **117**

Name: _____

What commas separate

■ Look for some sentences with commas. Write **five** in these boxes.

> Briefly, he scanned the food that lay before him.

>

>

>

>

>

■ What was the bit before the comma about?
How quickly he did it.

_____

_____

_____

_____

_____

■ What was the bit after the comma about?

What he did. Looking at food.

_____

_____

_____

Illustrations © 1999, Jane Cope.

PHOTOCOPIABLE

Sentences working together

Commas slot bits in

Sometimes we slot bits into sentences. Commas mark out the bits slotted in.

| Finally I found the shop. |

| Finally, after looking for hours, I found the shop. |

■ Cut these sentences between the commas and find the clause in the box that slots into the space you have made.

after searching for days	If you want,	, you can watch some telly.
with Sam's help	The mug,	, fell off the table.
which was full of juice	Joe yelled,	, "Catch me!"
as I get older	Do not,	, stroke the dog.
for any reason	I typed my story,	, on the computer.
who lives miles away	I found,	, the keys I lost last week.
after tea	My Gran,	, cycled to see me.
as he jumped off the wall	I find,	, my teeth are falling out.

Punctuation in writing

Objective

Apply punctuation in writing.

Writing focus

Children focus on the basic punctuation marks of a sentence and apply these to practical writing tasks.

Skills to writing

● Sentence by sentence

In the first stages of Key Stage 2, teaching should still be very focused on securing punctuated sentences. This needs to be worked through the whole-class' writing. All other punctuation marks flow from an understanding of the demarcated sentence. As children are writing, make sure they think sentence by sentence. Use that idea in shared, modelled and guided writing.

● Composition

The sentence is also a great tool for composition. Children need to learn that a good report unpicks its subject sentence by sentence; a good persuasive piece is built and a good story is told in the same way. When presenting a writing task, ensure children are thinking about the possible closing sentences as much as the earlier opening ones.

● Revision

Revisit writing to find the places where punctuation has been missed. Children can work in writing trios, where each child reads the writing of their team mates and particularly checks for punctuation possibilities and errors.

● Writing speech

Take every opportunity for writing speech. When writing news stories and non-fiction recounts, encourage children to put in and demarcate the speech of the participants. Every recount should be coupled with the question: *Who said what?*

● List threes

Commas for lists can be secured by encouraging children to think in threes. This is particularly effective for description. Characters can be tall, skinny and scary. Cottages can be small, old and quaint. The crucial piece of learning children need in order to demarcate such lists is that they need to count the items. Children will sometimes split items in a phrase with a comma (*I found chewing, gum, rubber, bands and money*). If they count the items they will see there are actually three items to be separated – not five words.

Activities

● Photocopiable page 122 'Speech bubbles'

The bubbles on the photocopiable sheet can be used to stimulate the devising of conversations. The model can be used in shared or guided writing. Children can contribute their thoughts about what participants say in the exchange, but once notes have been made they can then take this and write up the conversation in punctuated reported speech.

● Photocopiable page 123 'Word triangles'

Word triangles provide a way of gathering sets of three words around a theme written in the centre. For example, if they are describing something, children can write the noun at the centre then come up with an adjective for each angle. If they are making a list, they write the subject at the centre and list the nouns. These can be created as a preparation activity, with children planning their writing using the triangles to stimulate their word choice. Alternatively, they can be kept in a stash in the classroom to hand out to children who have completed a piece of writing. Give prompts such as: *I liked the goblin in your story but can you think of three adjectives to describe him?*

Write on

● **Waltz**

As a way of getting children into the flow of lists in sentences, come up with some waltz phrases. You can explain the 1, 2, 3 structure – and maybe even listen to some Strauss waltzes! The point is children can start to think in terms of 1, 2 and 3 for their descriptions (*big, green and very angry*) and other sentence lists. Devise some together, listening out for the 1, 2 and 3 structure.

● **Conversations**

Write the conversations of history. Find a historical topic that children have covered and write up, for example, the exchange Drake had as he was supposed to finish his bowls game and fight the Armada. Think of other topics of conversation that fit in with topic work.

● **Conversation acting**

To stimulate the writing of good speech, encourage children to act out exchanges in any text they may be writing. Working in twos, they can play out the argument two characters would have in a narrative they are writing. They don't need to rewrite the conversation word for word – far better that they listen out for and deploy the best lines in their text.

● **You will need…?**

Devise weird and wonderful 'You will need…' lists to accompany some strange tasks. What would you need to storm a pirate vessel or to cast a magic spell? From such questions children can devise their own 'You will need …' sentences, demarcating the items in their list.

● **Poetic commas**

Without stilting the creativity, it's worth using commas as a way of devising some good lines for use in poetry writing. If the poem is about the sun rising, then the *red, fiery sun* or the *round, angry sun* work well in the line. Similarly, if the poem is about an annoying brother, his *big, smirking face* will get on our nerves far more than an unqualified face.

What's on the CD-ROM

On the CD-ROM you will find:
● Printable versions of both photocopiable pages.

Name:

Punctuation in writing

Speech bubbles

■ Use the speech bubbles to draft a conversation between two characters.

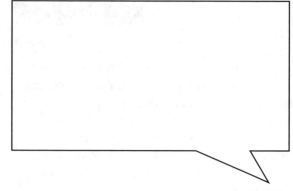

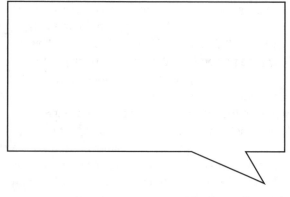

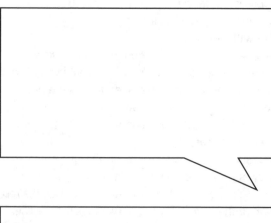

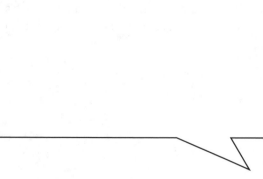

PHOTOCOPIABLE

SCHOLASTIC
www.scholastic.co.uk

Punctuation in writing

Word triangles

■ Write a noun in the centre of a triangle and gather adjectives around the angles. Then use the spaces under each planning triangle to devise descriptive sentences for your writing.

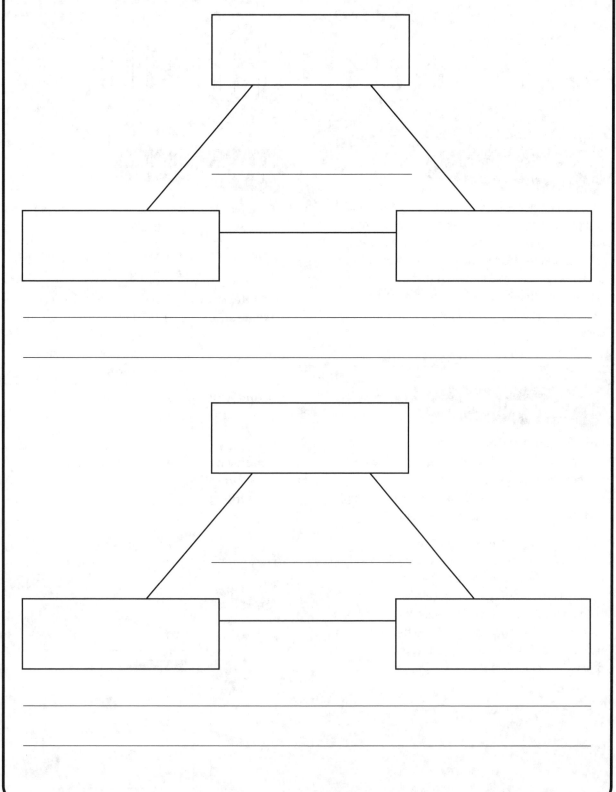

Chapter 6

Sentence writing and conjunctions

Introduction

The main emphasis in this chapter is on extending and developing sentence writing through connectives and particularly conjunctions. These are explored as structuring terms that order the passage of time in a text and also as devises that can join clauses. This then leads to work on the crafting of sentences, including a writing section on the use of conjunctions.

Poster notes

Conjunctions at work (page 125)
The various tasks conjunctions can perform are presented on this poster. The four categories can provide a way of children organising their learning and investigating examples of this word class.

Temporal conjunctions (page 126)
This poster will particularly support work in 'Working with sentences'. It provides a range of temporal conjunctions. These can be particularly useful to children involved in writing narrative text, whether it be a story or their own diaries. The different types of temporal conjunction can suggest ways of organising sentences.

In this chapter

Sentence writing and conjunctions

Conjunctions at work

Conjunctions can:

add one thing to another, for example: I like rain *and* I like snow.

oppose one thing against another for example: I like rain *but* my friend hates it.

show how one thing is linked to the time of another, for example: We put on warm clothes *so* we could go out in the snow.

show how one thing is caused by another for example: I like snow *because* it looks great.

Illustrations © 2008, Jane Cope.

Temporal conjunctions

Sentence writing and conjunctions

Illustrations © 2008, Jane Cope.

PHOTOCOPIABLE

Time words

Objective

Investigate how words and phrases signal time.

Background knowledge

Prepositions are words that indicate the link between things. For example, words like 'on' and 'beside' function as prepositions to say where one thing is in relation to another:

The vase is on the table.
The vase is beside the table.

One particular group of prepositions shows how things are linked in time:

We played before eating.
We played after eating.

This is a form of positioning, only in this case the prepositions indicate relative positions in time rather than space.

Other categories of words also indicate time, these include conjunctions and adverbs.

Activities

This section develops the understanding and use of a particular set of words and, in doing so, expands children's vocabulary. In such learning, children need to be given chances to think of examples of the type of word concerned and see where they could be used.

● **Photocopiable page 128 'Sequence'**
To rebuild the instructions for the yoghurt pot telephone, children will need to look at the temporal words used at the start of the various sentences.

● **Photocopiable page 129 'The tortoise and the hare'**
The story of the tortoise and the hare has already been used on photocopiable page 46 'Pronouns at play'. Children may want to use the script there to familiarise themselves with the story and dialogue before using this page to recount the tale.

● **Photocopiable page 130 'Recounted story'**
The boxes containing the temporal words can be used in various ways. Children could cut out all the boxes and:
   ● aim to use at least four in creating a story
   ● aim to use three selected by you in a particular order
   ● a group of five can take one each and create a group story.

Further ideas

● **Time word telling:** Time words (such as the ones used on photocopiable page 130 'Recounted story') can be written on cards and placed, face downwards, in the middle of a group of six children. The group then have the task of telling a story, sentence by sentence. One of them starts with an opening. The next one follows on, but first he or she must select one of the cards and then use the selected word as the starter for the sentence. This can send the story forwards, backwards, all over the place!

● **Preposition questions:** Children can quiz a child or an adult about the events of a previous day and try to come up with as many questions containing various temporal prepositions as they can think of, such as: *What did you do* after *breakfast? What were you reading* before *you sat in the classroom?*

What's on the CD-ROM

On the CD-ROM you will find:
   ● Printable versions of all three photocopiable pages.
   ● Answers to 'Sequence'.
   ● An interactive version of 'Sequence'.

Name:

Time words

Sequence

■ These instructions for making a 'yoghurt pot telephone' are jumbled up.
■ Cut out the boxes. Try putting the instructions back in sequence.

Then you thread one end of the string through one of the holes.

While one of you is speaking, the other listens at the other end.

First, you make a hole in the bottom of each yoghurt pot.

Meanwhile, your partner does the same with the other yoghurt pot.

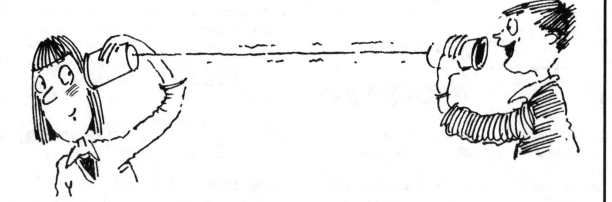

After you have threaded the string, you tie a knot.

Once you have threaded string through both ends, you stand apart.

When you are far enough from each other for the string to be slightly stretched, one of you speaks into your yoghurt pot.

Illustrations © 1999, Jane Cope.

PHOTOCOPIABLE

■SCHOLASTIC
www.scholastic.co.uk

Time words

The tortoise and the hare

■ Can you write the story using the opening words below?

Once... _____

So... _____

Then... _____

When... _____

Later... _____

So... _____

Meanwhile... _____

After... _____

Then... _____

In the end... _____

Name:

Recounted story

■ Write the title of your story in the box. Use the planning boxes and prepositions to help draft your story.

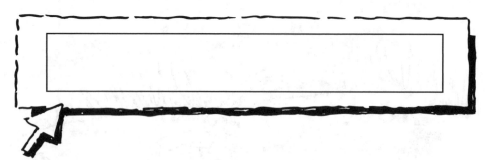

Story title

Once	Then	So
Meanwhile	In the end	After
When	Later	Before

Conjunctions

Objective

Use a wider range of conjunctions in extending sentences.

Background knowledge

Sentences can be simple, for example, *Joe made tea*. The simple sentence can be added to in a number of ways. Conjunctions are used to join together ('conjoin') two words, phrases or clauses. The word 'and' is the most common conjunction, joining words (*Joe made tea and coffee and juice*), phrases (*Joe made hot, sweet tea and black coffee and orange juice*) or clauses (*Joe likes tea and he likes coffee*). Conjunctions can:

● **add one thing to another:** *I like rain and I like snow.*

● **oppose one thing with another:** *I like rain but my friend hates it.*

● **show how one thing is caused by another:** *I like snow because it looks great.*

● **show how one thing is linked to the time of another:** *We put on warm clothes so we could go out in the snow.*

Activities

At this stage in their language development, children's learning about conjunctions will primarily involve understanding the job conjunctions do with a view towards using a variety in creating their own extended sentences.

● **Photocopiable page 132 'Join the sentences'**
As they join up the separated sentences on this photocopiable sheet, children will be guided by the conjunction that starts the second half of the sentence.

● **Photocopiable page 133 'Missing words'**
In choosing the right conjunction, children will need to consider the job that should be done in the space within each sentence. This will guide them to choose between, for example, a 'but' and a 'because'.

● **Photocopiable page 134 'Make the connection'**
The completion of the sentences in this activity is directed by the connective at the end of the opening section. Once they have completed the photocopiable sheet, children could try re-doing one of their completed examples with the conjunction altered (for example *I could eat you but…*, *I could eat you and…*).

Further ideas

● **Find examples:** Children can find a variety of words that connect one thing to another or show the relationship between one thing and another.

What's on the CD-ROM

On the CD-ROM you will find:
● Printable versions of all three photocopiable pages.
● Answers to 'Join the sentences' and 'Missing words'.
● Interactive versions of 'Join the sentences' and 'Missing words'.

Name:

Conjunctions

Join the sentences

■ Can you cut out and repair these broken sentences? Find a second clause to match every first clause.

■ Make a list of the words that join one half of a sentence with the other.

First clause	Second clause
I opened my umbrella	if you want them to grow.
We went to the library	because it was raining.
You need to water seeds	so I played on the slide.
Someone was on the swings	because the chain is broken.
We waited in the car	or a school dinner?
Joe looked for us	so I can buy a computer game.
I had my breakfast	until it is my birthday.
I can't wait	before I went to school.
Would you like sandwiches	and Lara went in goal.
I put on my sock	but it was closed.
We played football	after counting to fifty.
I can't ride my bike	before my shoes.
I have to save my pocket money	if you want to go out to play.
We got dressed	after doing PE.
Tidy the classroom	while Mum went in the shop.

Conjunctions

Missing words

■ Look at the spaces in these sentences. They are all words people said. They are real quotes.

■ Which words from the word box could fit? Write as many words as you think could fit in each space. Say them aloud to check if they sound right.

■ Try writing your own sentences using some of these conjunctions.

I had to go home ⬜ it was bedtime.

We didn't play outside ⬜ it was raining.

We had our sandwiches ⬜ we got on the bus.

I like juice ⬜ my mum likes tea.

We put water in the freezer ⬜ it turned into ice.

You can have a biscuit ⬜ some cake.

I have got a bike ⬜ it isn't working.

I haven't seen my friend ⬜ he moved house.

while	but	
	as	so
when	because	
		after
	or	
before	until	if

Illustrations © 1999, Jane Cope.

Name:

Conjunctions

Making the connection

- Can you finish these sentences? Fill in words you think the characters might say.
- List the words that connect the first part of each sentence to your added words.

I'm missing playtime because...

I told you to write a story but...

I like doing daring things although...

My old bike broke so...

I can sneak out when...

You can go out to play after...

I could eat you or...

I'll cast a spell on you if...

Illustrations © 1999, Jane Cope.

PHOTOCOPIABLE

Sentences making sense

Objectives

Develop awareness of longer sentences through experimenting with the deletion of words.
Understand the use of commas in longer sentences.

Background knowledge

In speech and writing, some words are more essential than others. We can précis a text down to essential words; something writers of notes do all the time. People who write reminders to themselves write the main words on a piece of paper (such as *Key – Sally Tues* as a reminder to *Give Sally the key on Tuesday*).

Certain words are essential to meaning; others can be deleted without losing the meaning of the sentence. However, these other words tend to help the sentence to read smoothly. These additional words make the difference between: *However, these other words tend to help the sentence to read smoothly* and *Other words help sentence smoothly*. Although the latter example makes sense, it is not a grammatical sentence.

The use of the comma in sentences indicates a pause between various items or clauses. In reading, the comma indicates that the reader pauses before reading on.

Activities

As children expand the length and vocabulary of the sentences they use and read, an understanding of the comma is important. Experimenting with deletion is one of the ways in which children can explore the information contained within a sentence.

● **Photocopiable page 136 'Word chopping'**
Through grasping the meanings of the sentences, children can decide which words to remove. Stress that they are trying to make the shortest sentence from those words. This will lead to differences as some decide, for example, that the words 'broken beyond repair' are all essential, while others feel it is sufficient to say 'broken'. For this reason, it is best if children work in pairs.

● **Photocopiable page 137 'Putting words into sentences'**
This activity builds up given words into a sentence. Within the given words there are some that will become the essential words in the sentence. Once they have written their sentences, children could try the previous word chopping activity on their own products and see which words can get the chop. Alternatively, they could pass their examples to a partner and see what words someone else would chop from their sentences.

● **Photocopiable page 138 'Commas in reading'**
The use of commas in this exercise is limited to the way they separate items in a list and separate the clauses in a sentence. The activity is best done as part of a discussion with children in which they have the opportunity both to read aloud and to hear passages from the text read out.

Further ideas

● **Telegrams:** Children can write messages about events to imaginary recipients far away. Once they have done this they have to try chopping the message down to the style of an old telegram. They will need some explanation as to what a telegram was and the way in which people used to use words sparingly in them.
● **Sentence strips:** Using sentences they have written, children can cut out the words they think are essential to the meaning and communication of the sentence.
● **Sentences chopped and back again:** In pairs, one child has to produce a sentence and chop as many words as they can from it, while retaining the meaning. They then hand this minimal version to their partner who has to rewrite the original. This can provide amusement when the originals are compared with the 'restoration' job done by a partner.

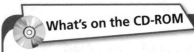 **What's on the CD-ROM**

On the CD-ROM you will find:
● Printable versions of all three photocopiable pages.
● Answers to 'Word chopping' and 'Commas in reading'.
● Interactive version of 'Putting words into sentences'.

Sentences making sense

Word chopping

■ Work with a partner. Cut out the sentences below. Take turns to read them and say what they are about. Once you have read them, try cutting words out of the strip while keeping a sentence that makes sense.

If the sentence says

Yesterday the little dog was scared by my aunty's motorbike.

we can cut out six words:

Yesterday | the | little | dog was scared | by my aunty's motorbike.

and the sentence still makes sense: | The dog was scared. |

On Tuesday we had a big party in the classroom.
The purple monster ate the purple fruit.
The thunder suddenly roared.
Our teachers made a fantastic new treehouse for us.
The little boat sailed down the fast stream.
Your cup of tea that was made half an hour ago is cold.
The big, old, spooky house is very cold.
The classroom ceiling light is completely and totally broken beyond repair.

Illustrations © 1999, Jane Cope.

PHOTOCOPIABLE   ■ **SCHOLASTIC**
www.scholastic.co.uk

Sentences making sense

Putting words into sentences

■ Put the words in each word box into a sentence. Use any other words you need to make the sentence. Make sure you include all the words in each word box in one sentence. Make a list of your sentences on a separate sheet of paper.

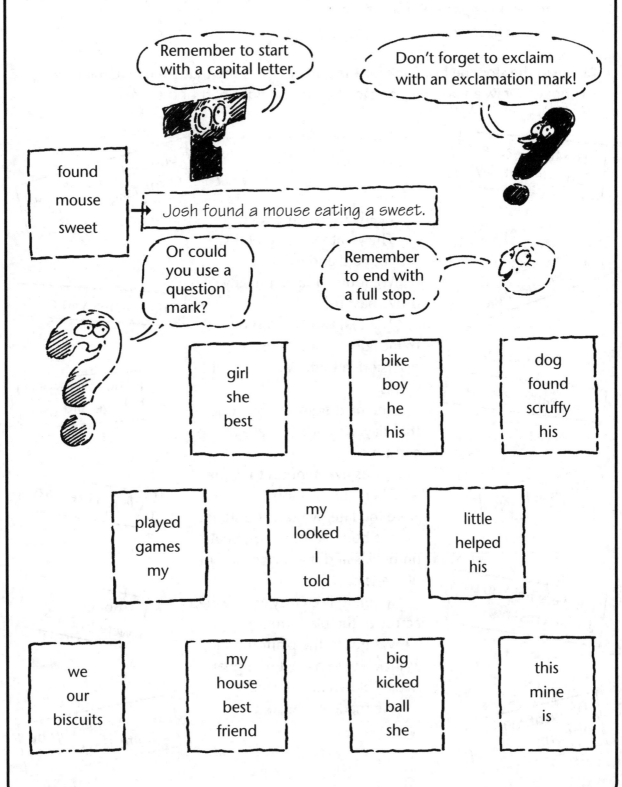

Remember to start with a capital letter.

Don't forget to exclaim with an exclamation mark!

found
mouse
sweet

→ Josh found a mouse eating a sweet.

Or could you use a question mark?

Remember to end with a full stop.

girl
she
best

bike
boy
he
his

dog
found
scruffy
his

played
games
my

my
looked
I
told

little
helped
his

we
our
biscuits

my
house
best
friend

big
kicked
ball
she

this
mine
is

Illustrations © 1999, Jane Cope.

SCHOLASTIC
www.scholastic.co.uk   **PHOTOCOPIABLE**   **Scholastic Literacy Skills**
                                                                          Grammar and punctuation: Year 3   **137**

Name:

Sentences making sense

Commas in reading

Two of the main uses of commas are:
- to separate items in a list
  The dog is short, smelly, scruffy and friendly.
- to separate parts of a sentence
  The dog, the smelly one, was friendly.

■ Read the story below. Look for the parts of the story that tell us the things in the boxes. Draw an arrow from each box to the right part of the story.

> The train was the last one that day.

> We bundled our umbrellas out of the taxi.

We nearly missed the train.

The weather was gloomy, drizzly, cold and wet.

We found a taxi, it nearly drove past us.

> We saw the station.

The taxi was held up by traffic lights, a level crossing, a diversion, a traffic jam and road works.

> The weather was cold.

The next train, the last one that day, was due to leave at eight o'clock.

It was five minutes to eight.

> The taxi nearly drove past us.

> The weather was wet.

Then, just as I thought we were too late, we saw the station.

We bundled our bags, coats, umbrellas and the pushchair out of the taxi.

> We were lucky.

> We ran like crazy.

Running like crazy, we dashed across to the platform.

We got to the platform and, as luck would have it, the guard hadn't blown his whistle.

We made it!

> We were held up by a level crossing.

> I thought we were too late.

> We went to the platform.

> We were held up by a traffic jam.

Working with sentences

Objective

Consolidate an understanding of sentences.

Background knowledge

Sentences can take many forms.
- **Simple sentences:** have a single clause that says one thing, such as: *The dog chased the cat*.
- **Compound sentences:** have two or more clauses that are equal in significance, linked by a conjunction like 'and' or 'then', such as: *The dog chased the cat and the cow jumped over the moon*.
- **Complex sentences:** have another clause which develops part of a simple sentence, such as: *The dog, having finished scratching his fleas, chased the cat*.
- **Minor sentences:** do not always look like sentences but, in a text, they stand alone and perform a function. Examples include: *Oh no!* and *Hello there!*

Activities

Teachers have found various ways of defining sentences for children. The problem is that some of these definitions are open to interpretation. Some definitions of a sentence are too technical to introduce to children of Key Stage 2 age. Teachers may have to rely on their instincts when deciding whether constructions which the children write are indeed sentences. The old-fashioned definition – that a sentence is capable of standing on its own and making sense – is a useful one.
- **Photocopiable page 140 'Strange sentences'**
Using the words on the photocopiable sheet, children have to try and write a sentence. They can aim to create the strangest sentence, possibly even voting on which one is strangest of all.
- **Photocopiable page 141 'Sentence starts, sentence ends'**
This activity develops children's growing awareness of when a sentence should start and finish. They have to try and find the points at which sentences will start and finish. Once they have done this, they can compare their results to see how they have judged starts and endings.

- **Photocopiable page 142 'Making sentences'**
As they place the lines of text shown on the photocopiable sheet into sentences, children will be faced with the task of creating some longer sentences than they may have encountered before. Some of the lines of text, such as *I can read*, are sentences in themselves. However, as they build new sentences out of such lines, they may start creating complex and compound sentences.

Further ideas

- **Depunctuate a text:** Looking at a text on the word processor, children can remove the punctuation. This will involve finding all the marks that demarcate the sentences in some way and deleting them or, in the case of capital letters, changing the case.
- **Sentence facts:** Children can look for things like the longest and shortest sentence they can encounter. They can draw on sayings and jokes to try and collect their favourite sentences, taking lines out of poetry and drawing on well known quotations.

What's on the CD-ROM

On the CD-ROM you will find:
- Printable versions of all three photocopiable pages.
- Answers to 'Sentence starts, sentence ends' and 'Making sentences'.
- Interactive versions of 'Sentence starts, sentence ends' and 'Making sentences'.

Working with sentences

Strange sentences

■ Look at the words in the word boxes and try to include each set of words in a sentence.

gorilla
slippers
ate

_____

_____

reading
singing
made

_____

_____

stopped
underwater
coat

_____

_____

moon
send
tree

_____

_____

teacher
dinner
purple
disgusting

_____

_____

found
turned
magic
coin

_____

_____

can
balloon
gone
animals

_____

_____

Working with sentences

Sentence starts, sentence ends

■ Look at these pieces of writing. There are no capital letters or full stops. Can you see the sentences in the passages?

■ Use colouring pencils to lightly shade over each sentence in a different colour.

last tuesday i went to
the park i played on the
swings my friend came
and played with me when
it was time to go i asked
my friend if she wanted
to come to my house my
friend said yes but first
she had to ask her mum
after she asked her mum
she came to my house she
stayed for tea

my mum did a parachute
jump she had never done
one before her friend dared
her to do it she was very
scared but she went to all
the lessons on the day of
her parachute jump we all
went to watch her we saw
her jump out of the plane
we waited and then her
parachute opened we were
so proud of her

once upon a time there was a
princess she lived all alone in a
big castle every day she went
to the market and bought two
baskets of fruit one basket

was full of apples the other
was full of oranges that was
all she had for breakfast
and dinner and tea

Illustrations © 1999, Jane Cope.

Name:

Working with sentences

Making sentences

- None of these lines of text has a capital letter or a full stop. Some of them could be sentences. Some are not.
- Cut out the lines of text and sort the ones that could be sentences from the ones that couldn't. Remember that a sentence stands on its own and says something.
- Look at the collection that do not make a sentence. Can you suggest sentences in which they would fit?

and in the room at the bottom of the stairs there was
can make a lot of things
we can read a book at the end of the day
I went to the jumble sale and bought some games
I can read
Serena didn't go straight home after school
so that was not a problem
look at this hole in the road
if we use all these boxes we can make a castle
on Tuesday we are going to
what do you know about a
the pirate lost his parrot

PHOTOCOPIABLE

Improving sentence writing

Objective

Write more extended sentences.

Writing focus

Drawing on the conjunctions, time words and the basic concept of the sentence, these activities teach children to reflect on the way sentences are structured with a view towards revising their own writing.

Skills to writing

● One sentence

This section is all about developing children's understanding of sentences as items that can be crafted, honed and refined. As they undertake writing tasks children can't do this fully for every sentence they write, but they can select one or two sentences from pieces they have written for polishing. Encourage the children at the end of their writing to select the sentence that they will review, thinking through the potential for a more powerful verb or the use of adjectives.

Children also need to check their sentences by asking *Does it read right?* Grammatical agreement is best developed by children reading aloud and checking that sentences sound OK.

● Temporal and causal

When reading and planning narrative, the two forms of conjunction should be highlighted. Clarify with the children the difference between temporal lines, where one thing follows another along a timeline, and causal connection, in which something like Cinderella's loss of a shoe is essential to the hunt that then takes place and resolves the story.

● Sequencing

Sequencing activities are important for children's grasp of story structure, as well as instructions and explanations. When doing these activities, point out to children the role played by conjunctions in structuring such texts.

● Complex times

Time words can be used to good effect as a way of encouraging children to write more complex sentences. Words like 'then' and 'while' immediately conjure up sentences with more than one clause. Children can be encouraged to think of sentences in which two things happen or two actions occur. The conjunctions 'because' and 'so' are particularly effective tools for structuring complex sentences.

● Instructions

When writing instructional texts, children should be encouraged to draw on a range of temporal conjunctions. Causal conjunctions can be highlighted as children encounter explanation texts, in which one phenomenon is caused by or causes another.

● Narratives and conjunctions

Use temporal conjunctions as a means of stimulating narrative writing. When planning a narrative task, draw children's attention to two conjunctions that may feature in their thinking and planning. For example, if the word 'because' is highlighted, children will think about the cause and effect of their plot, whereas a word like 'after' will stimulate them to think of the events that follow, one after the other.

Activities

● Photocopiable page 145 'Story stimulator'

The connecting words chosen on the planner provide children with some stimulation for their story writing. This should be used alongside regular planning and isn't a substitute for it. Structuring story notes that fall either side of, for example, the word 'because', children will be able to reflect on a causal connection in their planned narrative. Once they have completed the planner, children should read it through with a view towards whether any of the structures they have recorded stimulate addition to, or alteration of, their story.

● Photocopiable page 146 'Sentence crafting'

This photocopiable sheet is a tool for the revision process. Children select four sentences, either from texts they have written or read. They then think through whether they have punctuated them accurately or whether they could have used an alternative form of words. Could they have used an adjective or a better verb? Once they have asked these questions, they can revise their sentences in the box on the right.

Write on

● Conjunction trios

Working in 'conjunction trios' is a way of developing the use of conjunctions in writing. Each child takes a role. Child A acts as the conjunction, while the other two act as the parts of the sentence. Child B would be the part of the sentence before the conjunction and child C would be the part after it. So if the trio are working on a report about the school, child A may select 'so' as the conjunction. Child B will then think of something that could be written before 'so', such as *the bell rings*. Child C then has to think of something to come after the 'so', making a sentences like *The bell rings so we line up*. Children can take turns to play different parts in the three roles of the discussion.

● Sentence strips

Children can select words from a text they are writing or have written and copy them on a long strip of paper. They can then cut these up to change a word, insert adjectives, use a conjunction and extend the sentence or add a phrase followed by a comma.

● Why works

Children can use the word 'why' as a way of looking at the causal conjunctions that could be used in their writing. If they are planning a story they can consider why one thing caused another, if it's an instruction text they can ask why one action is needed in their task. The connections between one action and the other can be written on three-link paper chains, with the 'because' in the middle link and displayed by hanging them up in class.

● Random words

Children enjoy encountering and using new words. Every classroom should have a word of the week which is slightly more ambitious than regular spellings and that is discussed and tried out over the course of a week. Past words can be kept on display for children to refer back to.

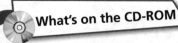

What's on the CD-ROM

On the CD-ROM you will find:
● Printable versions of both photocopiable pages.

Improving sentence writing

Story stimulator

■ Use this planner to devise ideas for a story. How could your story ideas be framed around these conjunctions? For example:

The candle went out **when** the window blew open.

	when	

	and then	

	so	

	because	

If	then	

SCHOLASTIC
www.scholastic.co.uk   **PHOTOCOPIABLE**   **Scholastic Literacy Skills**
Grammar and punctuation: Year 3   **145**

Name:

Sentence crafting

■ Write your original sentence in the left-hand column. Consider the prompts in the centre column and then write an improved sentence in the right-hand column.

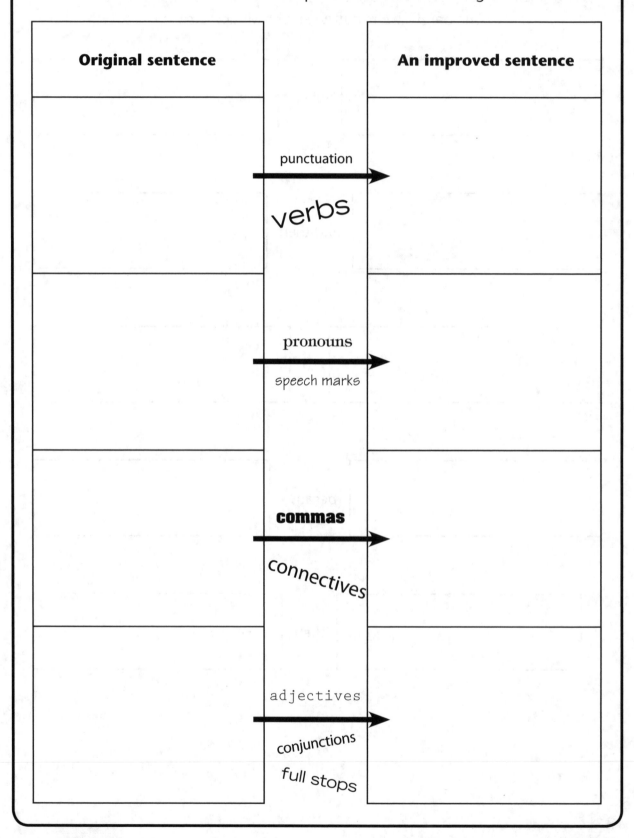

Original sentence		An improved sentence
	punctuation →	
	verbs	
	pronouns →	
	speech marks	
	commas →	
	connectives	
	adjectives →	
	conjunctions	
	full stops	

Subject knowledge

1. Preliminary notes about grammar

Grammar involves the way in which words of different types are combined into sentences. The explanatory sections that follow will include definitions of types of word along with notes on how they are combined into sentences.

Three preliminary points about grammar:
- Function is all-important. Where a word is placed in relation to another word is crucial in deciding whether it is functioning as a verb or a noun. For example, the word 'run' will often be thought of as a verb. However, in a sentence like *They went for a run*, the word functions as a noun and the verb is 'went'.
- There are some consistencies in the way spelling is linked to grammar. For example, words like 'play' and 'shout' have the '-ed' ending to make past tense verbs, 'played' and 'shouted'. Adjectives like 'quick' and 'slow' take a '-ly' ending to make adverbs like 'quickly' and 'slowly'. There are exceptions to these rules but such consistencies can still prove useful when it comes to understanding the grammar of sentences.
- Nothing is sacred in language. Rules change over time; the double negative has gained currency and regional variation in accent and dialect is now far more valued than has been the case in the past. The rules of grammar that follow are subject to change as the language we use lives and grows.

2. Words and functions

Grammar picks out the functions of words. The major classes or types of word in the English language are:

Noun
The name of something or someone, including concrete things, such as 'dog' or 'tree', and abstract things, such as 'happiness' or 'fear'.

Pronoun
A word that replaces a noun. The noun 'John' in *John is ill* can be replaced by a pronoun 'he', making *He is ill*.

Verb
A word that denotes an action or a happening. In the sentence *I ate the cake* the verb is 'ate'. These are sometimes referred to as 'doing' words.

Adjective
A word that modifies a noun. In the phrase *the little boat* the adjective 'little' describes the noun 'boat'.

Adverb

A word that modifies a verb. In the phrase *he slowly walked* the adverb is 'slowly'.

Preposition

A word or phrase that shows the relationship of one thing to another. In the phrase *the house beside the sea* the preposition 'beside' places the two nouns in relation to each other.

Conjunction

A word or phrase that joins other words and phrases. A simple example is the word 'and' that joins nouns in *Snow White and Doc and Sneezy*.

Article

The indefinite articles in English are 'a' and 'an' and the definite article is 'the'. Articles appear before nouns and denote whether the noun is specific (*give me the book*) or not (*give me a book*).

Interjection

A word or phrase expressing or exclaiming an emotion, such as 'Oh!' and 'Aaargh!'
The various word types can be found in the following example sentences:

Lou	saw	his	new	house	from	the	train.
noun	verb	pronoun	adjective	noun	preposition	article	noun
Yeow!	I	hit	my	head	on	the	door.
interjection	pronoun	verb	pronoun	noun	preposition	article	noun
Amir	sadly	lost	his	bus fare	down	the	drain.
noun	adverb	verb	pronoun	noun	preposition	article	noun
Give	Jan	a	good	book	for	her	birthday.
verb	noun	article	adjective	noun	conjunction	pronoun	noun

The pages that follow provide more information on these word classes.

Nouns

There are four types of noun in English.

> A **noun** is the name of someone or something.

Common nouns are general names for things. For example, in the sentence *I fed the dog*, the noun 'dog' could be used to refer to any dog, not to a specific one. Other examples include 'boy', 'country', 'book', 'apple'.

Proper nouns are the specific names given to identify things or people. In a phrase like *Sam is my dog* the word 'dog' is the common noun but 'Sam' is a proper noun because it refers to and identifies a specific dog. Other examples include 'the Prime Minister', 'Wales' and 'Amazing Grace'.

Collective nouns refer to a group of things together, such as 'a flock (of sheep)' or 'a bunch (of bananas)'.

Abstract nouns refer to things that are not concrete, such as an action, a concept, an event, quality or state. Abstract nouns like 'happiness' and 'fulfilment' refer to ideas or feelings which are uncountable; others, such as 'hour', 'joke' and 'quantity' are countable.

Nouns can be singular or plural. To change a singular to a plural the usual rule is to add 's'. This table includes other rules to bear in mind, however:

If the singular ends in:	Rule	Examples
'y' after a consonant	Remove 'y', add 'ies'	party → parties
'y' after a vowel	add 's'	donkey → donkeys
'o' after a consonant	add 'es'	potato → potatoes
'o' after a vowel	add 's'	video → videos
an 's' sound such as 's', 'sh', 'x', 'z'	add 'es'	kiss → kisses dish → dishes
a 'ch' sound such as 'ch' or 'tch'	add 'es'	watch → watches church → churches

Pronouns

There are different classes of pronoun. The main types are:

> A **pronoun** is a word that stands in for a noun.

Personal pronouns refer to people or things, such as 'I', 'you', 'it'. The personal pronouns distinguish between subject and object case ('I/me', 'he/him', 'she/her', 'we/us', 'they/them' and the archaic 'thou/thee').

Reflexive pronouns refer to people or things that are also the subject of the sentence. In the sentence *You can do this yourself* the pronoun 'yourself' refers to 'you'. Such pronouns end with '-self' or '-selves'. Other examples include 'myself', 'themselves'.

Possessive pronouns identify people or things as belonging to a person or thing. For example, in the sentence *The book is hers* the possessive pronoun 'hers' refers to 'the book'. Other examples include 'its' and 'yours'. Note that possessive pronouns never take an apostrophe.

Relative pronouns link relative clauses to their nouns. In the sentence *The man who was in disguise sneaked into the room* the relative clause 'who was in disguise' provides extra information about 'the man'. This relative clause is linked by the relative pronoun 'who'. Other examples include 'whom', 'which' and 'that'.

Interrogative pronouns are used in questions. They refer to the thing that is being asked about. In the question *What is your name?* and *Where is the book?* the pronouns 'what' and 'where' stand for the answers – the name and the location of the book.

Demonstrative pronouns are pronouns that 'point'. They are used to show the relation of the speaker to an object. There are four demonstrative pronouns in English 'this', 'that', 'these', 'those' used as in *This is my house* and *That is your house*. They have specific uses, depending upon the position of the object to the speaker:

	Near to speaker	Far away from speaker
Singular	this	that
Plural	these	those

Indefinite pronouns stand in for an indefinite noun. The indefinite element can be the number of elements or the nature of them but they are summed up in ambiguous pronouns such as 'any', 'some' or 'several'. Other examples are the pronouns that end with '-body', '-one' and '-thing', such as 'somebody', 'everyone' and 'anything'.

Person

Personal, reflexive and possessive pronouns can be in the first, second or third person.
- First-person pronouns ('I', 'we') involve the speaker or writer.
- Second-person pronouns ('you') refer to the listener or reader.
- Third-person pronouns refer to something other than these two participants in the communication ('he', 'she', 'it', 'they').

The person of the pronoun will agree with particular forms of verbs: 'I like'/'she likes'.

Verbs

The **tense** of a verb places a happening in time. The main three tenses are the present, past and future.

To express an action that will take place in the future, verbs appear with 'will' or 'shall' (or 'going to'). The regular past tense is formed by the addition of the suffix '-ed', although some of the most common verbs in English (the 'strong' verbs) have irregular past tenses.

> A **verb** is a word that denotes an action or a happening.

Present tense (happening now)	Past tense (happened in past)	Future tense (to happen in future)
am, say, find, kick	was, said, found, kicked	will be, will say, shall find, shall kick

Continuous verbs

The present participle form of a verb is used to show a continuous action. Whereas a past tense like 'kicked' denotes an action that happened ('I kicked'), the present participle denotes the action as happening and continuing as it is described (*I was kicking*, the imperfect tense, or *I am kicking*, the present continuous). There is a sense in these uses of an action that has not ended.

The present participle usually ends in '-ing', such as 'walking', 'finding', and continuous verbs are made with a form of the verb 'be', such as 'was' or 'am': *I was running* and *I am running*.

Auxiliary verbs

Auxiliary verbs 'help' other verbs – they regularly accompany full verbs, always preceding them in a verb phrase. The auxiliary verbs in English can be divided into three categories:

Primary verbs are used to indicate the timing of a verb, such as 'be', 'have' or 'did' (including all their variations such as 'was', 'were', 'has', 'had' and so on). These can be seen at work in verb forms like *I was watching a film*, *He has finished eating*, *I didn't lose my keys*.

Modal verbs indicate the possibility of an action occurring or the necessity of it happening, such as *I might watch a film*, *I should finish eating* and *I shouldn't lose my keys*.

The modal verbs in English are: 'would', 'could', 'might', 'should', 'can', 'will', 'shall', 'may', and 'must'. These verbs never function on their own as main verbs. They always act as auxiliaries helping other verbs.

Marginal modals, namely 'dare', 'need', 'ought to' and 'used to'. These act as modals, such as in the sentences *I dared enter the room*, *You need to go away* and *I ought to eat my dinner*, but they can also act as main verbs, as in *I need cake*.

Adjectives

The main function of adjectives is to define quality or quantity. Examples of the use of descriptions of quality include 'good story', 'sad day' and 'stupid dog'. Examples of the use of descriptions of quantity include 'some stories', 'ten days' and 'many dogs'.

> An **adjective** is a word that modifies a noun.

Adjectives can appear in one of three different degrees of intensity. In the table on page 152 it can be seen that there are '-er' and '-est' endings that show an adjective is comparative or superlative, though, as can be seen, there are exceptions. The regular comparative is formed by the addition of the suffix '-er' to shorter words and 'more' to longer words ('kind/kinder', 'beautiful/more beautiful'). The regular superlative is formed by the addition of the suffix '-est' to shorter words and 'most' to longer words. Note, however, that some common adjectives have irregular comparatives and superlatives.

Nominative	Comparative	Superlative
The nominative is the plain form that describes a noun.	The comparative implies a comparison between the noun and something else.	The superlative is the ultimate degree of a particular quality.
Examples	**Examples**	**Examples**
long	longer	longest
small	smaller	smallest
big	bigger	biggest
fast	faster	fastest
bad	worse	worst
good	better	best
far	farther/further	farthest/furthest

Adverbs

Adverbs provide extra information about the time, place or manner in which a verb happened.

> An **adverb** is a word that modifies a verb.

Manner Provides information about the manner in which the action was done.	Ali *quickly* ran home. The cat climbed *fearfully* up the tree.
Time Provides information about the time at which the action occurred.	*Yesterday* Ali ran home. *Sometimes* the cat climbed up the tree.
Place Provides information about where the action took place.	*Outside* Ali ran home. *In the garden* the cat climbed up the tree.

Variations in the degree of intensity of an adverb are indicated by other adjectives such as 'very', 'rather', 'quite' and 'somewhat'. Comparative forms include 'very quickly', 'rather slowly', and 'most happily'.

The majority of single-word adverbs are made by adding '-ly' to an adjective: 'quick/quickly', 'slow/slowly' and so on.

Prepositions

Prepositions show how nouns or pronouns are positioned in relation to other nouns and pronouns in the same sentence. This can often be the location of one thing in relation to another in space, such as 'on', 'over', 'near'; or time, such as 'before', 'after'.

Prepositions are usually placed before a noun. They can consist of one word (*The cat* in *the tree...*), two words (*The cat* close to *the gate...*) or three (*The cat* on top of *the roof...*).

> A **preposition** is a word or phrase that shows the relationship of one thing to another.

Connectives

The job of a connective is to maintain cohesion through a piece of text.

Connectives can be:

- Conjunctions – connect clauses within one sentence.
- Connecting adverbs – connect ideas in separate sentences.

> A **connective** is a word or phrase that links clauses or sentences.

Conjunctions

Conjunctions are a special type of connective. There are two types: coordinating or subordinating.

Coordinating conjunctions connect clauses of equal weight. For example: *I like cake and I like tea.* Coordinating conjunctions include: 'and', 'but', 'or' and 'so'.

Subordinating conjunctions are used where the clauses of unequal weight, they begin a subordinate clause. For example: *The dog barked because he saw the burglar.* Subordinating conjunctions include: 'because', 'when', 'while', 'that', 'although', 'if', 'until', 'after', before' and 'since'.

Name of conjunction	Nature of conjunction	Examples
Addition	One or more clause together	We had our tea *and* went out to play.
Opposition	One or more clauses in opposition	I like coffee *but* my brother hates it. It could rain *or* it could snow.
Time	One or more clauses connected over time	Toby had his tea *then* went out to play. The bus left *before* we reached the stop.
Cause	One or more clauses causing or caused by another	I took a map *so that* we wouldn't get lost. We got lost *because* we had the wrong map.

Connecting adverbs

The table below provides the function of the adverbs and examples of the type of words used for that purpose.

Addition	'also', 'furthermore', 'moreover', 'likewise'
Opposition	'however', 'never the less', 'on the other hand'
Time	'just then', 'meanwhile', 'later'
Result	'therefore', 'as a result'
Reinforcing	'besides', 'anyway'
Explaining	'for example', 'in other words'
Listing	'first of all', 'finally'

3. Understanding sentences

Types of sentence
The four main types of sentence are declarative, interrogative, imperative and exclamatory. The function of a sentence has an effect on the word order; imperatives, for example, often begin with a verb.

Sentences: Clauses and complexities
Phrases
A phrase is a set of words performing a grammatical function. In the sentence *The little, old, fierce dog brutally chased the sad and fearful cat*, there are three distinct units performing grammatical functions. The first phrase in this sentence essentially names the dog and provides descriptive information. This is a noun phrase, performing the job of a noun – 'the little, old, fierce dog'. To do this the phrase uses adjectives.

Sentence type	Function	Examples
Declarative	Makes a statement	The house is down the lane. Joe rode the bike.
Interrogative	Asks a question	Where is the house? What is Joe doing?
Imperative	Issues a command or direction	Turn left at the traffic lights. Get on your bike!
Exclamatory	Issues an interjection	Wow, what a mess! Oh no!

The important thing to look out for is the way in which words build around a key word in a phrase. So here the words 'little', 'old' and 'fierce' are built around the word 'dog'. In examples like these, 'dog' is referred to as the **headword** and the adjectives are termed **modifiers**. Together, the modifier and headword make up the noun phrase. Modifiers can also come after the noun, as in *The little, old, fierce dog that didn't like cats brutally chased the sad and fearful cat*. In this example 'little, 'old' and 'fierce' are **premodifiers** and the phrase 'that didn't like cats' is a **postmodifier**.

Phrase type	Examples
Noun phrase	The *little, old fierce dog* didn't like cats. She gave him *a carefully and colourfully covered book*.
Verb phrase	The dog *had been hiding* in the house. The man *climbed through* the window without a sound.
Adjectival phrase	The floor was *completely clean*. The floor was *so clean you could eat your dinner off it*.
Adverbial phrase	I finished my lunch *very slowly indeed*. *More confidently than usual*, she entered the room.
Prepositional phrase	The cat sat *at the top of* the tree. The phone rang *in the middle of* the night.

The noun phrase is just one of the types of phrase that can be made.

Notice that phrases can appear within phrases. A noun phrase like 'carefully and colourfully covered book' contains the adjectival phrase 'carefully and colourfully covered'. This string of words forms the adjectival phrase in which the words 'carefully' and 'colourfully' modify the adjective 'covered'. Together these words, 'carefully and colourfully covered', modify the noun 'book', creating a distinct noun phrase. This is worth noting as it shows how the boundaries between phrases can be blurred – a fact that can cause confusion unless borne in mind!

Clauses

Clauses are units of meaning included within a sentence, usually containing a verb and other elements linked to it. *The burglar ran* is a clause containing the definite article, noun and verb; *The burglar quickly ran from the little house* is also a clause that adds an adverb, preposition and adjective. The essential element in a clause is the verb. Clauses look very much like small sentences, indeed sentences can be constructed of just one clause: *The burglar hid, I like cake*.

Sentences can also be constructed out of a number of clauses linked together: *The burglar ran and I chased him because he stole my cake*. This sentence contains three clauses: 'The burglar ran', 'I chased him', 'he stole my cake'.

Clauses and phrases: the difference

Clauses include participants in an action denoted by a verb. Phrases, however, need not necessarily contain a verb. These phrases make little sense on their own: 'without a sound', 'very slowly indeed'. They work as part of a clause.

Simple, compound and complex sentences

The addition of clauses can make complex or compound sentences.

Simple sentences are made up of one clause, for example: *The dog barked, Sam was scared*.

Compound sentences are made up of clauses added to clauses. In compound sentences each of the clauses is of equal value; no clause is dependent on another. An example of a compound sentence is: *The dog barked and the parrot squawked*. Both these clauses are of equal importance: 'The dog barked', 'the parrot squawked'. Other compound sentences include, for example: *I like coffee and I like chocolate, I like coffee, but I don't like tea*.

Complex sentences are made up of a main clause with a subordinate clause or clauses. Subordinate clauses make sense in relation to the main clause. They say something about it and are dependent upon it, such as in the sentences: *The dog barked because he saw a burglar*; *Sam was scared so he phoned the police*.

In both these cases the subordinate clause ('he saw a burglar', 'he phoned the police') is elaborating on the main clause. They explain why the dog barked or why Sam was scared and, in doing so, are subordinate to those actions. The reader needs to see the main clauses to fully appreciate what the subordinate ones are stating.

Subject and object

The **subject** of a sentence or clause is the agent that performs the action denoted by the verb – *Shaun threw the ball*. The **object** is the agent to which the verb is done – 'ball'. It could be said that the subject does the verb to the object (a simplification but a useful one). The simplest type of sentence is known as the SVO (subject–verb–object) sentence (or clause), as in *You lost your way*, *I found the book* and *Lewis met Chloe*.

The active voice and the passive voice

These contrast two ways of saying the same thing:

Active voice	Passive voice
I found the book.	The book was found by me.
Megan met Ben.	Ben was met by Megan.
The cow jumped over the moon.	The moon was jumped over by the cow.

The two types of clause put the same subject matter in a different voice. Passive clauses are made up of a subject and verb followed by an agent.

The book	was found by	me.
subject	verb	agent
Ben	was met by	Megan.
subject	verb	agent

Sentences can be written in the active or the passive voice. A sentence can be changed from the active to the passive voice by:

- moving the subject to the end of the clause
- moving the object to the start of the clause
- changing the verb or verb phrase by placing a form of the verb 'be' before it (as in 'was found')
- changing the verb or verb phrase by placing 'by' after it.

In passive clauses the agent can be deleted, either because it does not need mentioning or because a positive choice is made to omit it. Texts on science may leave out the agent, with sentences such as *The water is added to the salt and stirred*.

4. Punctuation

Punctuation provides marks within sentences that guide the reader. Speech doesn't need punctuation (and would sound bizarre if it included noises for full stops and so on). In speech, much is communicated by pausing, changing tone and so on. In writing, the marks within and around a sentence provide indications of when to pause, when something is being quoted and so on.

Punctuation	Uses	Examples
A	**Capital letter** 1. Starts a sentence. 2. Indicates proper nouns. 3. Emphasises certain words.	All I want is cake. You can call me Al. I want it TOMORROW!
•	**Full stop** Ends sentences that are not questions or exclamations.	This is a sentence.
?	**Question mark** Ends a sentence that is a question.	Is this a question?
!	**Exclamation mark** Ends a sentence that is an exclamation.	Don't do that!
" " **' '**	**Quotation (speech) marks** **(or inverted commas)** Encloses direct speech. Can be double or single.	"Help me," the man yelled. 'Help me,' the man yelled.
,	**Comma** 1. Places a pause between clauses within a sentence. 2. Separates items in a list. 3. Separates adjectives in a series. 4. Completely encloses clauses inserted in a sentence. 5. Marks speech from words denoting who said them.	We were late, although it didn't matter. You will need eggs, butter and flour. I wore a long, green, frilly skirt. We were, after we had rushed to get there, late for the film. 'Thank you,' I said.
—	**Hyphen** Connects elements of certain words.	Co-ordinator, south-west.
:	**Colon** 1. Introduces lists (including examples). 2. Introduces summaries. 3. Introduces (direct) quotations. 4. Introduces a second clause that expands or illustrates the meaning of the first.	To go skiing these are the main items you will need: a hat, goggles, gloves and sunscreen. We have learned the following on the ski slope: do a snow plough to slow down… My instructor always says: 'Bend those knees.' The snow hardened: it turned into ice.

Punctuation	Uses	Examples
;	**Semicolon** 1. Separates two closely linked clauses, and shows there is a link between them. 2. Separates items in a complex list.	On Tuesday, the bus was late; the train was early. You can go by aeroplane, train and taxi; Channel tunnel train, coach, then a short walk; or aeroplane and car.
'	**Apostrophe of possession** Denotes the ownership of one thing by another (see page 159).	This is Mona's scarf. These are the teachers' books.
'	**Apostrophe of contraction** Shows the omission of a letter(s) when two (or occasionally more) words are contracted.	Don't walk on the grass.
...	**Ellipsis** 1. Shows the omission of words. 2. Indicates a pause.	The teacher moaned, 'Look at this floor... a mess... this class...' Lou said: 'I think I locked the door... no, hang on, did I?'
( )	**Brackets** Contains a parenthesis – a word or phrase added to a sentence to give a bit more information.	The cupboard (which had been in my family for years) was broken.
—	**Dash** 1. Indicates additional information, with more emphasis than a comma. 2. Indicates a pause, especially for effect at the end of a sentence. 3. Contains extra information (used instead of brackets).	She is a teacher – and a very good one too. We all know what to expect – the worst. You finished that job – and I don't know how – before the deadline.

Adding an apostrophe of possession

The addition of an apostrophe can create confusion. The main thing to look at is the noun – ask:

- Is it singular or plural?
- Does it end in an 's'?

If the noun is singular and doesn't end in 's', you add an apostrophe and an 's', for example: Indra's house the firefighter's bravery	**If the noun is singular and ends in 's'**, you add an apostrophe and an 's', for example: the bus's wheels Thomas's pen
If the noun is plural and doesn't end in 's', you add an apostrophe and an 's', for example: the women's magazine the geese's flight	**If the noun is plural and ends in 's'**, you add an apostrophe but don't add an 's', for example: the boys' clothes the dancers' performance

Further reading

Carter, R; Goddard, A; Reah, D; Sanger, K; Bowring, K (2001) *Working with Texts: A Core Book for Language Analysis* (second edition), Routledge

Crystal, D (2004) *Rediscover Grammar* (second edition), Longman

Crystal, D (2003) *The Cambridge Encyclopedia of the English Language* (second edition), Cambridge University Press
A big volume but very accessible, covering many areas of English including grammar, punctuation and dialect. Filled with interesting asides and examples from sources as varied as Shakespeare to Monty Python.

Hurford, JR (1994) *Grammar: A Student's Guide*, Cambridge University Press
An excellent text, setting out basic guidelines on the workings of grammar.

Sealey, A (1996) *Learning About Language: Issues for Primary Teachers*, Open University Press
A more theoretical work that presents some of the issues and arguments surrounding knowledge about language.

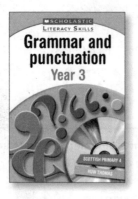

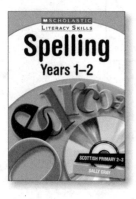

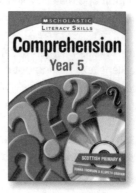
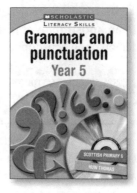
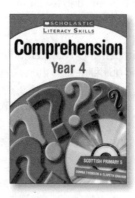

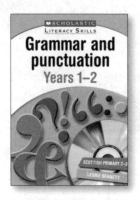

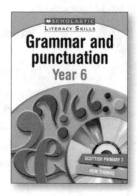

■■SCHOLASTIC

Also available in this series:

Grammar and punctuation Years 1–2
ISBN 978-1407-10045-6

Grammar and punctuation Year 3
ISBN 978-1407-10046-3

Grammar and punctuation Year 4
ISBN 978-1407-10047-0

Grammar and punctuation Year 5
ISBN 978-1407-10048-7

Grammar and punctuation Year 6
ISBN 978-1407-10049-4

Spelling Years 1–2
ISBN 978-1407-10055-5

Spelling Year 3
ISBN 978-1407-10056-2

Spelling Year 4
ISBN 978-1407-10057-9

Spelling Year 5
ISBN 978-1407-10058-6

Spelling Year 6
ISBN 978-1407-10059-3

Comprehension Years 1–2
ISBN 978-1407-10050-0

Comprehension Year 3
ISBN 978-1407-10051-7

Comprehension Year 4
ISBN 978-1407-10052-4

Comprehension Year 5
ISBN 978-1407-10053-1

Comprehension Year 6
ISBN 978-1407-10054-8

To find out more, call: 0845 603 9091
or visit our website www.scholastic.co.uk